Living by Memories

TULASI ACHARYA

Published by Mantra Publication, 2022.

LIVING BY MEMORIES

First edition. October 4, 2022.

ISBN: 979-8215846803

Written by TULASI ACHARYA.

Living

by

Memories

A collection of brilliant articles on society, culture, politics, human nature, memories, and much more.

By **Tulasi Acharya**

Section: One

(A collection of articles on society, culture, politics, human nature, memories, art, and Literature, and much more.)

Turning the Focus on Students

LAST MONTH, THREE MEMBERS of the Nexus Institute of Research and Innovation (NIRI), including myself, were invited as guest speakers at an interaction programme organised by a higher secondary school in Nepal. We were to talk about the existing teaching practices in Nepal and America, the differences, and the tools and techniques one could introduce in Nepali classrooms to make teaching more effective, innovative, scientific and career-oriented. The focus of the interaction revolved around the research-based method of the student-centred classroom that has yet to be practiced when it comes to discussions about teaching in Nepal. At the programme, even the participant lecturers from colleges in Nepal realised that student-centred teaching was the need of the hour.

Tara Sigdel, associate professor of surgery at Stanford University, California, reflected on the teacher-centred practice in Nepal where students relied completely on what their teachers said. But the model has yet to be changed, he said. He reflected on American teaching practices that are just the opposite, such as encouraging students to interact in the classroom, ask critical and rigorous questions, work in groups, and solve problems. Similarly, Tika Lamsal, associate professor of English at the University of San Francisco, underscored the idea of student-centred teaching by introducing Paulo Freire's "banking concept of education" that challenges the idea of teachers being wisdom-filled vessels who lecture and students being empty vessels who just receive what the lecturers give. Such teaching hinders the intellectual growth of students by turning them into, metaphorically speaking, comatose "receptors" and "collectors" of information that often have no real connection with their lives and lived experiences.

Based on my 20 years of teaching experience, I believe it is high time to introduce more student-centred teaching methodology in the classroom. One doesn't need highly equipped classrooms, computer labs and plentiful infrastructure to practice student-centred teaching. There are a few things one can bring in to make the classroom student-centred, and many start with attitudes and what teachers see as the end goal of teaching.

Guru-disciple dichotomy

The idea of a guru who knows everything creates a dichotomy: A teacher as someone who is authentic, reliable and knows the truth; and a student as a disciple who doesn't know a lot, cannot question the teacher, cannot counterargue, and is just a passive listener. When one breaks the citadel of this mindset and mentality and lets everyone know that the teacher is a facilitator, students can be active agents participating in discussions, bringing in critical questions, observing, counterarguing and presenting facts based on reliable research and sources. This will motivate students to actively participate in discussions and makes the class interactive. This will even motivate and challenge the teacher to keep abreast of up-to-date information, so they start reading and researching, and trashing old notebooks from which they have been letting their students copy for years. Learners will come to realise the world is very complex and that there is not a single truth to fully rely on.

Now let's introduce the flipped classroom teaching method. In this method, the teacher frontloads the students giving them a discussion topic with sources for them to explore before they come to the classroom. Students come to the class fully prepared and having researched and read the matter. They present their ideas individually or in a group, and the teacher sits in the back listening to their ideas. The teacher asks questions that help clarify misperceptions and helps students think more critically about their assumptions and conclusions.The teacher is a facilitator and motivator. To teach well, teachers must first know their students' interests, strengths and struggles. Knowing the students helps teachers plan and teach with prior knowledge of what will help them succeed or hinder them. A writing teacher, for example, may ask the students on the first day of class to provide a writing sample from which they can discover their interest in a topic, writing skills and so on. Teachers must give their students autonomy and get them into the habit with structured guidelines for peer review, where students work on their topics with a group that their teacher helps them form. Similarly, introducing media literacy and showing students the value of using smartphones, not just for the purpose of scrolling Facebook, but to present ideas and publish them on applications is necessary.

Academic qualifications

One gets a degree at an educational institution. That degree should not be only of academic qualifications, but represent the student's moral integrity, creativity faculty and potential skills. Student-centred teaching debunks the idea of students as only receptors, and emphasises the idea of their being researchers and explorers with skills and potential to solve problems. Each student is unique. They have talents and abilities, and the job of teachers is to find them within the students and let them build and explore—in multiple curriculum areas. In student-centred learning, undue emphasis is not given to the textbook and its contents, but encourages students to challenge the textbook from the title to the end page. The whole world is an open textbook, and teachers can help their students explore, observe, form perspectives, create knowledge and contribute to the existing store of knowledge.

No student or teacher enters the classroom as a blank slate. The students come from different socio-linguistic and cultural backgrounds, and each of them deserves to share their life experiences equally, and they are equally enriching in the classroom. Education is not only to obtain a certificate or degree, but also to know the society and its people, know the social values, think outside the box, and be humble, accountable and responsible. If the teaching practices in the classroom cannot encourage students to be active learners, go outside and research, come to the classroom and teach, and reflect on what they have learned and how they have learned it, the students will always remain passive, and they will fail to understand how their world works. They will fail to contribute to the development of the nation. (***Published in The Kathmandu Post dated September 5, 2022***)

Translating Nepali Literature in English

ALONG WITH THE PUBLICATIONS of different genres, one can experience a plethora of translation[1] of Nepali writings into another language, especially English. According to Padam Prasad Devkota[2] (2022), "The bulk of Nepali literature in English consists of translations and original compositions in English." Adhikari[3] (2016) writes, "As to English-Nepali translation, it's almost a century-old phenomenon. Nepali-English translation, on the other hand, has only crossed five decades. Shyam Das Vaisnav's collection of poems Upahar is the first Nepali literary writing to be translated into English. Laxmi Prasad Devkota translated it under the Present in 1963." Although there were some translations in the time of Laxmi Prasad Devkota who himself translated many of his books and others into English, there was not enough amount of translation. *Muna Madan* was first translated **in 1970. Some of Devkota's English translations were also published in *Indreni*, a poetry magazine then.** Many of the books by different writers were translated later, such as Pallav Ranjan's translation of Devkota's "The Pilgrims" (1995), Madhav Prasad Ghimire 's "Ashwatthama" (1998), Parijat's novel, "Blue Mimosa," (1972), Diamond Shamsher's "The Wake of the White Tiger," (2011) Bharat Jangam's "The Black Sun," (1990), and so on.

Current translation

---

1. https://en.wikipedia.org/wiki/List_of_Nepali_literature_in_English

2. https://creativenepal.co.uk/contemporary-literature-in-english/

3. http://eltchoutari.com/2016/12/translation-should-be-used-as-a-technique-not-a-method-in-elt-balram-adhikari/

Most recently, there are many literary works being translated into English, such as Padmavati Singh's "Parallel Sky," Govinda Raj Bhattarai's "Muglan," and BP Koirala's "Narendra Dai," Niraj Bhattarai's "Threads of Smoke," Bhisma Upreti's "Kathmandu Kaleidoscope," Sanjeev Upreti's "Another Cultivation of Maize," Krishna Dharabasi's "Radha," Chuden Kabimo's "Song of the Soil," Buddishagar Chapai's "Karnali Blues," or the coming out soon ones, such as Nayan Raj Pandey's "Ular," Amar Neupane's "Seto Dharti" and the list goes on and on. If one looks at the proliferation of translations currently, Acharya[4] (2020) writes that the future of Nepali literature and its English translation is promising.

Future of translation

According to Hodgkinson[5], chair of the judging panel for the 2020 International Booker Prize "Much of the most exciting, playful and inventive new fiction can be read in translation." If the translation fails to bring in such playfulness in writing, whether original or translated, it fails to woo the reader. Hodgkinson looks for "compulsive stories, haunting characters, a finely tuned voice" that makes one see the world afresh. But with translated fiction, he further adds there are several added dimensions, such as whether a translator is making to evoke a "distinctive authorial sensibility in English."

On this note, one can notice that most of the fictions that have been awarded international literary prizes carry such playfulness and freshness in writing, for example, Marieke Lucas Rijneveld's *The Discomfort of Evening* or the most recent International Booker Prize Winning novel, a translated one, *Tomb of Sand* by Gitanjali Shree.

---

4. https://samayasamachar.com/2020/02/23/nepali-literature-its-promising-future-and-translation/

5. https://fivebooks.com/best-books/the-best-of-world-literature-the-2022-international-booker-prize-shortlist-frank-wynne/

Both bring playfulness in writing. The former gives a lot of details that the readers themselves feel being in the dairy farm. It portrays the rural life so beautifully and the relationship with the family and family members. The latter reflects on mother-daughter, parent-child relationship. The reader can glimpse the translator's grasp of Shree's exultant word play and hear the original Hindi cadence of the novelist. It shows that the success of the good translation of a novel or writing a novel in its original form can be measured in terms of the characters' lives and relationships, playfulness of language, and making the story come to life. That also might be the reason why Buddisagar's *Karnali Blues,* a story about the relationship of son and father, have drawn the attention of many readers and have also been translated into English by Michael Hutt. In the interview by Flyn[6] (2020), Hodgkinson says, "a fine translator can calibrate your ear to the inflections and nuances that make a character come to life. A good translation captures the idiosyncrasies of the original novel without being slavishly literal. It enters the creative spirit of the author's vision."

Despite some challenges, regarding the future hope of translation, Abhi Subedi[7] (2019), "The lure of English is also associated with the new energy. Some Nepali writers write with near-native proficiency. Some well-known among them live abroad. There is a great interest in translating Nepali literary works, especially poetry, into English to reach out to the wider readership. But there are problems in this direction. Apart from a few good translations, this euphoria could give the opposite picture of Nepali literature. But the efforts of individuals and organizations are underway."

Challenges

6. https://fivebooks.com/best-books/the-best-of-world-literature-the-2022-international-booker-prize-shortlist-frank-wynne/

7. http://lifeandlegends.com/nepali-literature-dialogic-relation-between-criticism-and-history-by-abhi-subedi/

Translation is difficult if one fails to handle the original text in its own culture. It is more than a literal one. Our cultures and cultures are composed of many overlapping stories that the translations need to be wary of. In a video "The Danger of a Single Story," a novelist Chimamanda Adichie[8] (2009) tells the story of "how she found her authentic cultural voice—and warns that if we hear only a single story about another person or country, we risk a critical misunderstanding." Again, Hodgkinson[9] says, "A good translation makes it possible for you to enter these worlds without any profound cultural knowledge of the places that you're going to, though you might acquire it as you go. A good translation enables that journey and renders you fluent in another culture." A good translation makes the reader feel familiar and something innovative at the same time. In this context, Yashee[10] (2022) gives an example and writes, "one of the reasons to pick up *Ret Samadhi*, or *Tomb of Sand*, is its refreshing wisdom and cadence, which will feel new and familiar at the same time." Until one brings such cadence, playfulness, and profound cultural knowledge in writing, it will be very hard for Nepali writing—whether in English or translated into English—to enter the cannons of Nepali writing in English. Bala Ram Adhikari[11], who holds a Ph.D. in translation and, also, teaches and does translations opines translation as "a technique, not a method."

Conclusion

Translation is a difficult task to do. It demands a lot of hard work and research. It wants the translator to walk in the shoes of the original

---

8. https://www.youtube.com/watch?v=D9Ihs241zeg&t=1s

9. https://fivebooks.com/best-books/the-best-of-world-literature-the-2022-international-booker-prize-shortlist-frank-wynne/

10. https://indianexpress.com/article/books-and-literature/tomb-of-sand-international-booker-prize-3-reasons-to-read-7944344/

11. http://eltchoutari.com/2016/12/translation-should-be-used-as-a-technique-not-a-method-in-elt-balram-adhikari/

writer and the society the writer lived. Therefore, a good translation of a good book is a must. Translation should not only be of language translation, but the translation of ideas and emotions that must conveyed effectively through dialogue, description, and details. Also, translation in as many languages as possible can broaden the wider readership. To gain wider readership of Nepali literature it is to best translate the best writing that brings in voices of the marginalized into English and other languages and make them available in many digital platforms globally so any reader across the world will have access to. Nepali literature still is waiting for good translation. In this context, publishers should encourage to not only focus on translating Nepali to English or English to Nepali with an idea that it would help our literature and culture travel, but also should focus on translating other languages into Nepali for Nepali literature to grow more. International literary organizations and the organizations like NRNA (Non-Resident Nepali) should equally play a crucial role for good translations of Nepali literature. Mahesh Paudyal (2019),[12] a critic and translator, writes about the importance of translation for Nepali writing to receive more attention and visibility in the world. (***Published in the Rising Nepal dated September 2, 2022***)

---

12. https://glli-us.org/2019/11/16/nepali-literature-needs-more-attention-and-visibility-in-the-world-an-interview-with-author-translator-mahesh-paudyal/

Discourse on Sex in Nepal

THE MORE WE HEAD TOWARDS the civilised world, the more we hear news about rape cases, sexual abuse and harassment. Nepal's Facts Research and Analytics, the study of the Human Rights Commission and other miscellaneous police reports also show that incidents of rape are increasing. Looking at data from the United Nations, rape cases are growing globally. Especially in a patriarchal country like Nepal, the cases are even higher. Why is such horror rampant and hidden within the so-called civilised society even today?

Two Incidents

Here are two incidents to begin with in this article. First, while working for an organisation that worked for people with disabilities, a thirty-five-year-old man with a disability told as if he was going to rape someone right away, "I want to have sex with a woman." The statement was a challenge to those who thought a person with a disability would have no sexual desire, but what was shocking was not what he said, but how he said it—his statement carried a sort of deep-down anger much more than the love. One could contemplate his sexual desire—perhaps it was because he has never had sex in his life, and, as a result, that turned into a sort of latent anger and depression.

Second, a tourist— who one night in Nepal encountered a sex worker who took his money and ran away, and he again reached out to another one the very next day and managed to have sex with her— said with a fully satisfied look, "This time I even enjoyed having sex venting all my anger and frustration I got from the one who took my money and ran away last night." Listening to him, one could be dumbfounded: what sort of sex it was—so dull and depressed, filled with anger and revenge that didn't carry love and feelings at all. Isn't the highest point of the sexual act the deepest love in the making, the meeting of two souls, and the physical, mental, and psychological satisfaction that different books on sex, such as the Kamasutra talks about?

Rape, gang rape, child rape, kidnap and rape, teacher raping student, father or grandfather raping daughter or granddaughter and similar scandals have been heard very frequently in news. One of those scandals in the context of Nepal, for example, is the Nirmala rape scandal and the recent Sushmita Scandal.

When such news stories are out, they make anyone's hair stand on its end and make them act immediately either by hanging the rapist or cutting his penis. But will such punishment be given to the rapists to prevent the rape from happening? Before this question is answered, the discourse on sex in Nepal needs to be discussed.

Rapes Increasing

If one looks at the increasing rape incidents in Nepal, it can be since sex is viewed as a filthy topic to talk about— especially since the patriarchal society has a mindset that perceives sex as a very uncivilised and dirty topic to bring up. Thus, sex becomes merely a tool to dominate, deride, loathe, disrespect, and humiliate the person, especially women. Nepali society is very pretentious in this matter—the society that has been watching and reading miscellaneous sexual positions and postures of gods and goddesses that have been chiselled out on the wooden Hindu temples in Kathmandu and discussed in the Kamasutra as pious and religious finds the discussion of sex or the act of kissing between the partners in public deviant, uncivilized, and perverted.

Such a pretentious society considers Madan Rai, an agriculturalist and social scientist, a pervert when he talks about sex openly on social media. They deride Rai, saying, "Perverted Rai is going to ruin Nepali society and the prestige of Rai community." Society doesn't want to bother with the interpretation of healthy sex and its relationship with human quality of life, but rather does keep it as a topic of shame to discuss.

Whether that be an incident of Draupadi— a single wife of five Pandava brothers in the Mahabharat story— who was made naked in public in front of her husband, or be the incident during the Rana era when the husband was tortured by making his wife and forcing her to walk along the city naked. What this shows, especially in the South Asian context, is that a woman's sex is more of a thing attached to a family's prestige or dignity rather than it should have been the act of optimum point of love or an indispensable biological need that has an important relationship with a quality life.

Such discourse on sex in the Nepali context has created a rhetoric of sex and sexual activity in such a way that one understands sex as a means just to procreate children only, otherwise that must be kept secret and hidden. Nepali society unconsciously has defined and used sex as a tool of punishment or as a means of taking revenge, venting anger and frustration, and stripping the woman and her family of her prestige. Such a deep-rooted discourse of sex in Nepali society has prevented many of them from making and understanding the connections between sex and sexual activities to the significance of human quality of life.

Rhetoric Of Sex

In a patriarchal society like Nepal, such rhetoric below builds elusive psychology on men that abet them to rape.

1. "When a woman says 'no,' 'no', that means she is saying 'yes,' 'yes'": At times boys in their early twenties are heard talking about their girls. One says, "I tried so hard, but she kept saying 'no,' 'no'. And his friend

next to him says, "she is pretending, you know. She wants you. You must try harder."

Such rhetoric is the outcome of a patriarchal society that has already shaped the understanding of men over females' bodies, resulting in rapes. C. Muehlenhard, L. C. Hollabaugh's research article "Do women sometimes say no when they mean yes? The prevalence and correlates of women's token resistance to sex" shows that when women say "no" that means "no." It is because they have been looking for the guarantee of intimacy and love, not because they didn't have sexual desire. When a man ends up having sex without the woman's acceptance, that becomes rape, which leaves a long-term trauma upon the woman.

2. "I am a man, dude": This is another rhetoric the patriarchal society has created. The impression it has left is that being a man is not to be a woman, but rather to demonstrate "manliness," which means a man can marry as many women as possible. Even society stamps on the certificate of his manliness if he has more than one wife. Society defines man in terms of his anger, pride, revenge, and revolt, while women are defined in terms of the word like passive and tolerance like earth. Such discourse and rhetoric encourage rape in society.

3. "What a beauty she is—look at her slim body, big chest, beautiful butt, and pretty face. This type of language defines the beauty of a woman that lies more in her appearance than her inner talents. Such beauty is advertised everywhere from the world of glamour to literature, film, and advertisement to beauty pageants. Such projections of women prevent sex and sexual activities from understanding from the perspective of love, feelings, sympathy, and sensitivity. Gender-biased pop culture and stereotypes have marginalised women, resulting in many rape cases.

Again, most rape incidents are the outcomes of such discourses that look at sex as a topic of taboo, as a matter of the person's and the person's family's prestige. Especially in the context of Nepal, when sex is attached to the woman's dignity, two things come into play: I) sex is attached to the woman's dignity and that encourages men to rape her without her acceptance if he wants to kill her dignity. II) since the woman's dignity is connected to her family's prestige, the family doesn't want to bring the case up even if it becomes aware of the rape and it, therefore, encourages the rapist even more.

Understanding of Sex

In conclusion, the unhealthy understanding of sex in the context of Nepal has encouraged rape. When sex is understood only in terms of the relationship between penis and vagina, it abets rape. When society fails to mete out equal power to all sexes and acknowledge the importance of their equal participation, it encourages rape.

As patriarchal society continues to think that venting anger and frustration against women, killing her moral dignity and family prestige, and taking revenge and ridiculing her is the only way through having non-consensual sex, it inspires multiple incidents of rape.

When one fails to understand the meaning of sex and its relationship with human quality of life, when one fails to acknowledge the significance and indispensability of sex in one's life, when one cannot incorporate the biological need for sex in living beings and when one cannot treat sex as the optimum point of love and intimacy, sympathy, humanity, and as the meeting of two souls, rapes continue to take place.

Madan Rai writes a status on his Facebook wall: "Let's remove the idea of female dignity imposed onto her vagina. Vagina must be transparent; it is not a hidden topic." Until a healthy understanding of sex replaces the current cultural discourse and rhetoric of sex in Nepal, no punishment will stop the rape incidents.

In the name of civilisation, it is a curse that society has failed to understand sex as the most important part of healthy and quality life and has rather perceived sex and sexual activities as uncivilised and filthy demeanour. Robert McRuer and Anna Mollow in their book "sex and disability" write that sex is the most important part of quality life. Let's respect it, without making it a topic of shame and stop the rape incidents to occur frequently. (***Published in the Rising Nepal dated July 29, 2022***)

Emerging Nepali Writers in English

TRACING THE HISTORY of Nepali English writing is difficult. However, Swechcha (2019) writes, "Padma Jung Bahadur Rana's The life of Sir Junga Bahadur Rana, a biography in English of the first Rana Prime Minister of Nepal, made the solid path for coming generations to venture into English."

Going back to the history of Nepali writing in English or Nepali writers writing in English, there is not a solid date as such because a person or two might be writing in English sporadically that never came into notice until— especially talking about the cannons of Nepali writing in English— the publication of Manjushree Thapa's Mustang Bhot in Fragments (1992) or The Tutor of history (2001) or Samrat Upadhyay's Arresting god in Kathmandu (2001), an anthology of short stories. Pro. Ammar Raj Joshi, Vice chancellor of Mid-Western University and a scholar of English, raised a question in his keynote in a program "Nepalese English Writers' conference" first time organized by VIEW (Village of English Writers) in Chitwan—what should be the right category for the writing in English originally written by Nepali writers? Should that be "Nepali writers in English" or "Nepalese writing in English" or "English written by Nepali writers?" The speakers later emphasized that both original writing in English and Nepali translated into English could go under any category irrespective of the terminologies we use. The prominent question is: what is the emerging situation of Nepali English writing and its global reach in international literary market?

The publications of Thapa and Upadhyaya's books seem to have declared the entry of Nepali writing in English or Nepali writers writing in English. In a review of Mustang Bhot in Fragment that was published in the Rising Nepal a long time ago, Durga Prasad Bhandari highlighted the advent of a very good English writer in Nepali literary scene (Swechcha, 2019). When Samrat Upadhyaya came up with his first book Arresting God in Kathmandu, it garnered good reviews and accolades. According to Mulmi (2017), "Although literature in Nepal has a long history, Nepali writing in English (NWE) only caught international attention in the early 2000s, after the publication of Manjushree Thapa's The Tutor of History and Samrat Upadhyay's Arresting God in Kathmandu." After the publication houses swarmed into India and Arundhati Roy's 'The God of Small Things' won a Booker prize in 1997 when it was published, Swechcha (2019) writes, "The English-speaking world started looking up at South Asian English writing from a different perspective. Nepal being close to India, danced then to the tune of Indian English writing that was taking the world by storm."

According to Padma Prasad Devkota, the youngest son of Laxmi Prasad Devkota, Nepalese writing in English can be noticed from Laxmi Prasad Devkota's two works of English: Bapu and Other Sonnets, Shakuntala, which were originally written in English during the 1950s. Along with that, Devkota has also written criticism, stories, and essays in English. In fact, Devkota has laid the foundation of writing literary works in English. According to Pun (2017), "After Laxmi Prasad Devkota pioneered Nepali writing in English in the 1950s, Mani Dixit, Tek Bahadur Karki, Abhi Subedi, Padma Prasad Devkota, D.B. Gurung, Laxmi Devi Rajbhandari, Peter J Karthak, Rishikesh Upadhyaya, and a few others continued to write in English during the 1960s, 70s and 80s." Currently— despite the renowned ones like Thapa and Upadhyaya— we have many writers writing in English, some examples include Sushma Joshi, Rabi Thapa, Sheeba Shivanagini Shah, Ajit Baral, Richa Bhattarai, M.K. Limbu, Yuyutsu Sharma, Ishwor Kandel, Tulasi Acharya, Niranjan Kunwar, Prawin Adhikari, Khem Aryal, Aditya Man Shrestha, and so on. Even the publication of La.Lit, a literary magazine edited by Rabi Thapa has contributed a lot to Nepalese English writing. This reflects on the emerging trend of Nepali writers writing in English. Mulmi (2017) writes, "Indian publishers such as Speaking Tiger are commissioning new work, and publications like La.Lit and The Record are doing all they can to encourage Nepali writing in English."

The recent publications of Nepali writing in English by younger writers seem to be contributing to the cannons of Nepalese writing in English, despite the fictional works of Manju Shree Thapa and Samrat Upadhyaya. Some of the examples could be Rabi Thapa's short story collection Nothing to Declare and his non-fiction Thamel: Dark Star of Kathmandu, Prawin Adhikari's The Vanishing Act, Pranaya Rana's City of Dreams, Shraddha Ghale's The Wayward Daughter, and Greta Rana's Hostage that have been received exceptionally well. On top of that, Prajwal Parajuly's Land Where I Flee (2014) and Niranjan Kunwar's Between Queens and the Cities (2021) have received excellent feedback. Between Queens and the Cities, a book of non-fiction, is even able to bring in the marginalized voice of a Nepali gay man, a new and fresh perspective into play.

Such emerging Nepalese writers in English will help cross the border of linguistic, cultural, and geographical boundaries while helping Nepalese writing enter the cannons of Nepali writing in English. Sahitya Post (2020) writes, "Along with the proliferation in its theme and style, Nepali literature written in either language also has multifaceted objectives in its creation. Issues of ethnicity, socio-cultural structures, identity, roots, and diaspora have become the mainstream." With that said, one can assume that the Nepalese writing in English is promising. However, Nepali writing in English is yet to bring in the "unheard melodies" of the marginalized in a unique way, except for Kunwar's Between Queens and the Cities that highlights a struggle of a gay man from Nepal.

Although we have Samrat Upadhyaya's novels in English published from outside of Nepal, they are yet to be published by publishers like Simon and Shuster and HarperCollins and be featured in the New Yorker. On top of that, still some critics are wary of Upadhya's fictions for their wrong projection of Nepali society, culture, and women. Nepali times (2003) writes, "Samrat looks all set to continue packaging Nepalis as solely governed by their libidinal drives, with Manjushree patting him on the back." The emerging writers in English must be cognizant of all these critics while writing in English and help Nepali English travel across the world and enter the cannons of Nepali writing in English. In an interview by Robertson (2022), Shrestha says, "If Indian English is acceptable, then why isn't Nepali English, Nigerian English, or Singaporean English?" This shows that we should let Nepali English writing reach out to wider audience whether that be the writing in English originally or Nepali translated into English. Without being exotic, we must be honest in writing to bring in unique and innovative content that carries original sensibilities and idiosyncrasies that the audience in the global market are looking for. Talking about the emerging Nepali writers in English, best translations of best Nepali writing in English is also equally important that help cross the border of linguistic, cultural, and geographical boundaries. (***Published in the Kathmandu Post dated July 8, 2022***)

Sex Among Older People

THE DESCRIPTION OF sex or sexual activities in the Kamasutra, a sex manual written by Vatsyayana, and ancient Indian philosopher, displays the significance, praise, and power of sex, and its quality relationship with human life. However, the more significant and praiseworthy sex appears to be the discussion of older people's sexual lives or the sexual lives of people with disabilities.

As people with disabilities are deemed as people with no sexual desire, the sexual desire of older people can be considered the butt of a joke. It is because older people are connected to the idea of people with a disability as they are also deemed to be physically challenging, incapable or feeble.

Without Sexual Desire?

Thus, our society finds older people as disabled who are also without sexual desire. Our society tends to connect physical feebleness with mental, emotional, and psychological feebleness and concludes that older people are without sexual desire.

Robert Mcruer and Anna Mollow's "Sex and Disability," Don Kulick and Jens Rydstrom's "Loneliness and It's opposite," Tom Shakespeare's "The Sexual Politics of Disability," and Michael Gill's "Intellectual Disability and Sexual Agency" discuss the significance of sex and its importance for a quality life of people. However, they discuss how people are parochial and biased at the idea of sex, especially, when it comes to the sex lives of people with disabilities.

Our society also puts older people into the category of people with disabilities and discourages their sexual lives. "It is because our society connects the feebleness of older people with physical incapacities of people with disabilities," says Krishna Murari Gautam, the founding principal of "Ageing Nepal" in Kathmandu, who has been researching and writing about older people for a long time.

In a society that defines people with disabilities as people with no sexual desire, who will realise the importance of sex in the lives of older people? Who will help better understand the significance of sex and its relationship with the quality of life of people?

The significance of sex lies not only in the lives of adults but also does lie in the lives of older people. According to the World Health Organisation (WHO), to be healthy sexually is the stage when the person is completely healthy physically, mentally, emotionally, and socially. When one represses the sexual desire, then it will reduce one's quality and rhythm of life. In the article "Factors Conditioning Sexual Behaviour in Older Adults: A Systematic Review of Qualitative Studies" published in the Clinical Medicine Journal, Cano et al (2020) write that healthy sex is required for the person's complete life experience, especially for those who are fifty or fifty plus.

The article further mentions that sexual activities among the older population are an important part of their quality lives that are related to their mental and physical health while establishing a satisfying relationship in their lives and preventing them from different chronic diseases. If one fails to fulfil sexual needs, one will suffer from depression, pessimism, loneliness, and others, which may cause one to act aberrantly in their behaviour of sexual practices.

There is always a lack of sexual experience among people with disabilities and older people. It is because either they might have not been living as married couples or might have lost their partners who they could have sex with. It is also because society looks down upon the sexual practices among older people and people with disabilities, and, therefore, fails to understand their sexual needs.

No Partners

According to the Census 2022 of Nepal, more than thirty hundred thousand of the population is sixty plus. Among them, some of them are living a life without a partner since they never married or might have lost their partner.

Those who remarried could be men more than women because of the prevalence of our patriarchal society that still looks down upon the widow getting married.

Our society is not open to talking about sex and its significance. In a general survey among people of sixty plus, most of the participants reflected on the parochial patriarchal society that didn't let them, first, talk about sex openly, second their age factor prevented them from talking about sex, and third, sex is defined only in terms of sexual intercourse.

In the article "Sex Life of Older People: Self-Reported Sexual Activity in Australian Sexagenarians," published in Clinical Research Journal, Jason A Ferris, Anthony M A Smith, et al. (2008) write that an active sexual life is very important for a person's good health. In the survey, more than 90 per cent accepted the significance of sex with human health.

Most of the survey questions asked to the respondents had to do with physical pleasure and physical and emotional satisfaction. According to health doctors, no matter what the person's age is, sex is always connected to the person's healthy life. In "The Secrets of Life of Older People That Can Make Us Rethink Our Idea of Intimacy," Sharron Hinchliff (2015)' points out that those who are older than seventy seem to have had sex more than three times a month while some of them do not even reply due to their coyness.

The article even mentions that those who have had sex seem to have experienced a quality life compared to those who didn't. In the article "Sex in the Senior Years," Mark Stibich (2022) writes that many people think that as people get older, they lose sexual interest and desire, and they become less important.

Although there might be some truth in it, the survey was done by the University of Michigan (2017) shows that forty per cent of people from age between 70 to 80 seem to have been in active sexual activities. This shows that there does lie the significance of sex. As people get older there might be some problems, as a few health experts point out, such as taking time for erection (for men), dryness of the vagina (for women) and so on. However, the biggest hindrances in active sexual activities are the social attitudes towards sex, sex lives of older people, lack of social awareness, deep-rooted social and cultural taboo, and biased social and cultural understanding of sex, some older people explain. In one of the surveys done by Lee, Nazroo, et al. (2016) in Britain shows that 60 per cent are engaged in active sexual activities among 70- to 80-year-old people, and 33 per cent are from 80 to 90 years old.

However, the less are women. And the reason is not that they have no sexual desire, but because they have no opportunity for sex, the study shows. Kalra et al (2012) writes, "Human beings are never too old to enjoy a happy and healthy sex life."

Deeper Relationship

In the article "Sexual Activity Among Seniors: What Is Normal?" published in the Huffington Post (2017), it is mentioned that out of 7000 participants, only 3 per cent didn't want to say anything, but most of them said that they were sexually active even at the age of eighty. In the article "We Slept with Hundreds of People: Three Older Women on Sex and Pleasure" published by the Repeller, Iman Hariri-Kia (2019) writes that sex is an activity between two people that makes their relationship deeper and qualitative."

It is, therefore, to say older people have no sexual desire is an illusion and false. According to Cano et al (2020), there is always sexual desire among older people, and they can utilize it properly. Cano et al further say that some older people have even better sex lives than when they were adults, especially those who are not under social and familial pressures. This infers that sometimes social and cultural taboos about sex, sexual biases, religious prejudices about sex, and the question of morality regarding sex interfere with the quality of people's sexual lives.

Similarly, in the article "Frequency of Sexual Intercourse Among Residence of Bangladesh, India, and Nepal" published in the Journals of Psychosexual Health, Yasir Arafat et al.(2021) writes about the physical relationship with human health, but we fail to understand that way when it comes to the sexual activities of older people. Especially, in the context of Nepal, if one's partner passes away, we discourage one to remarry, especially if she is a woman, due to the biased social attitudes toward the widow that links to cultural taboo.

Again, if the person is a woman, poor, and from a lower caste, it will be unimaginable for our society to think on behalf of the marginalized ones' sexual needs and desires. The more the person is marginalized, the less one thinks about the person's capacity to have sex.

In the land that sowed the Kamasutra, the same land shies away from the talk of sex. Even the kissing between a husband and wife in public becomes the question of morality, let alone the talk of the Kamasutra. Society looks down upon the talk of sex and sexual needs and human bodily needs.

On the one hand, we have the Kamasutra, a sex manual, and on the other hand, the talk of sex and public participation on the topic is almost unknowingly prohibited. The society that considers sex taboo tells us to forget about the relationship of Vishwamitra and Menaka in the forest and the chiselled-out sexual postures of Gods and Goddesses in the temple.

One should not forget that the significance of sex comes with the quality of life. Robert Mcruer and Anna Mellow (2012) writes that "Sex and quality of life are interdependent." However, we continue to make this topic taboo and impose our ethos that people with disabilities and older people have almost no sexual desire.

We continue to create such rhetoric that prevents many people from living a quality life while controlling their emotional and psychological aspects of life, and, eventually, create a discourse that encroaches on the biological rights of older people and people with disabilities.

Quality Life

In "History of Sexuality," Michael Foucault (2012) writes that such biased rhetorical discourses prevent us from questioning authority and seeing things outside the box. We must know sex and its significance in human lives, whether the person is an adult or older or has a disability.

In this context, Tom Shakespeare, the author of "Sexual Politics of Disability" is very open and writes that if those who want sex but are incapable to have it, it will be better to find a sex worker for them so they can fulfil their sexual desire. It is not a question of morality or immorality; it is a question of whether the person is living a quality life or not. (*Published in the Rising Nepal dated July 8, 2022*)

Embrace Ethical Leadership

THE RESULTS OF LOCAL elections have come out letting us know what happens if political parties fail to address people's concerns and local problems. Mainly, the winning of Balen Shah as Mayor of Kathmandu Metropolitan City, Harka Sampang of Dharan Sub-metropolitan City and Gopal Hamal of Dhangadi Sub-metropolitan City — all of them were/are independent candidates — give a clear message that people can simply refuse to elect someone from the institutionalised parties if the latter fail to establish a good relationship with them through communication, cooperation, and cooptation. This election is a reminder that people are power that can place or displace the leader who fails to deeply think of people's agendas and meet their mandates.

Those who seem to have worked on behalf of people in the past have been reelected even this time, for example Chiribabu Maharjan from Lalitpur Metropolitan City and Renu Dahal from Bharatpur Metropolitan City. This also shows that people are not illiterate or incorrigible or without a conscience when it comes to the time of election. One should not undermine the power of people who are ready to give a lot of benefits of doubt until the leader realises it.

There is a reason why this local election gave us a surprise. It is not because people completely lost the trust in the political parties. They simply give a jolt to the parties when the latter stick to status quo. The election results are also the outcome of, to some extent, people's frustrations with the political parties, but more than that they seem to have focused on the candidates' clear agendas and the existing and immediate problems the candidates were able to bring up during election times instead of wasting their time and energy blaming the opposition party and the party leaders.

Ethical leadership

Most of the political leaders in the past failed to bring in ethical leadership that is important for a positive change in the society. Thus, all the winners from the local elections must introduce ethical leadership during their tenure if they want the people to continue to trust them.

According to Philip Selznick, when we define leadership, it should be defined in terms of social and institutional contexts to create congruence between the leader and the follower, between the what the leaders do and how the followers perceive. To create such congruency, the leader should value sociological and psychological characteristics from society, for example how society functions, how people in the society behave, and how society is made, while infusing day to day behaviour with long-run meaning and purpose.

The leader is a statesman, becoming critical of internal and external pressures and identifying the socio-cultural structure based on social beliefs, cultures, myths, and personal narratives, and how they affect the structure of the institutions, organisations, and ministries. A leader with the knowledge of ethical leadership will be cognizant of these. If there is a lack of ethical leadership, it affects leader-follower relationship, impelling people not to trust the leader at all. The leaders must have the knowledge of the culture, people, and the context people live in, and the leaders should be guided by positive attitudes for doing something for the society.

Ethical leadership has moral guidance as it does the right things and does things right. The ethical leadership is path finding and culture building, facilitating institutional learning. Ethical leadership is more guided by the elements of conservatorship leadership that emphasises the understanding of tradition and culture. Emphasising the importance of culture, ethical leadership restricts any incongruence from happening, and enhances institutional or societal positive change through What Mathew Dull would say "control, competence, and commitments." In this case, the leaders' dialogue and communication with the local people become very important in understanding a culture and how that culture can alter decision making and improve performance in the society.

An understanding of how society is built is the key in ethical leadership. The leader must be able to recognise the social biasness. The leader should be willing to think for the broader interest of people. The leader that has many good followers help society to grow, bring coordination, cooperation, and cooptation in the organisation and social reformation. Ethical leadership is about knowing the core values, individual identities, marginalized narratives and their lived experiences, vision, virtue and learning from them organisational/institutional norms, values, and principles. Knowing the institutional values leads to the rituals of confidence and good faith, which legitimatise the work the leaders do by establishing good relationships between the leader and the follower and creating congruence within the working culture. The leader who lacks ethical leadership will be driven by over ambition, pride and bragging.

Positive change

Ethical leadership is crucial in understanding the personal narratives and social, cultural, mythical, and psychological aspects of the society. Ethical leadership works to address the uncertainties and helps create congruency between the leader and the follower. It helps the leader to be critical of and design the leadership structure and principle and help the society grow and build the trust between people and the leaders accordingly. Thus, ethical leadership really matters for a positive change in the society and to have people to continue to trust the leader. Those who represent us, no matter which political party they belong to, must introduce ethical leadership in their deeds.

The local elections results must be the opportunity to end the habits of blaming each other and start reviewing critically where they failed and how they failed to bring in ethical leadership in their work, behaviour, and attitudes that will only lead them to be a better leader in the future. This message is also for those who have been winners in this election. If they fail to bring in ethical leadership and move forward, we can imagine what might happen. (***Published in The Rising Nepal Dated June 1, 2022***)

The Nepali Literary Environment

NEPALI LITERATURE HAS recently progressed by leaps and bounds compared to the time of the Rana regime, especially when it comes to writing different genres, translating them, and reflecting on the voices of the marginalised in the works of literature. In this article, I have given the Keatsian term "unheard melodies" to the voices of the marginalised. Here, the marginalised means subalterns, such as women, Dalit, people with disability, the poor, the illiterate, and people from different ethnic and cultural backgrounds who have never been heard, and the like. Nepali literature has yet to reach its height in terms of its efficacy to bring the "unheard melodies" of the marginalised who have unique socio-cultural and ethnic and religious and geographical experiences that the audiences in the global world are looking forward to reading and researching.

THE 104-YEAR-LONG RANA regime (1846-1951) prevented writers from writing for the laypeople, let alone the voices of the marginalised. Writing remained in praise of the Rana regime or the people in power. Literature became the genre belonging to the societal elite. Social change through writing was a far cry. Krishna Lal Subba was imprisoned for nine years for writing a book entitled Makaiko Kheti (1920), meaning "the cultivation of maize". According to Devendra Pandey, Subba was "deemed to be trying to influence collective thinking of the Nepali people on the possibilities of social change that the then regime would not allow".

Control and censorship

The Gorkha Language Publication Committee was established in 1913 to control and censor publications. If anyone wishes to publish a book on any topic, he must first bring it to the Gorkha Language Publication Committee for inspection. If a book is published without the committee's approval, the publisher will be fined fifty rupees. If the content of the book is improper, the book will be seized, and punishment will be meted out according to the committee's decision.

However, towards the end of the Rana regime, Michael Hutt writes, "Some writers had started rejecting the classical conventions of the older tradition, others adapted traditional genres and styles to express new concerns."

In this run, Laxmi Prasad Devkota's Muna Madan (1936) became (and is still now) the most popular book, a literary genre, a genre of the marginalised that depicted the society of that time and the lives of the commoners, their daily chores, and love and humanity.

Despite some other genres, such as dramas by Bal Krishna Sama and others, the most flourishing genre then was poetry. The poets then were very active, conscious and revolutionary, such as Dharanidhar Sharma, Mahananda Sapkota, Surya Bikram Gyawali, Siddhicharan Shrestha, Laxmi Prasad Devkota and many others. Poetry became the medium of expression, as we see in the poetry of Bijaya Malla, Mohan Koirala, Ramesh Bikal and Bhupi Serchan during the 1960s and 1970s. However, the poetry genre alone couldn't address the conditions of the marginalised.

The Nepal Academy was established in 1957 to develop and promote Nepali literature. However, the establishment of the Panchayat system and its one-language policy deterred the development of literature in many languages that lasted from 1960 to 1990, which means the opportunity to bring in the voices of the marginalised from different ethnic, linguistic and cultural backgrounds remained a distant shore.

Sajha Prakashan, a government-owned publishing house, began operations in 1964. Some works of fiction and non-fiction in the Nepali language were published. During the 1960s, younger writers were influenced by existentialism, Marxism, and Freud, but their prevailing tone was social and cultural alienation rather than political rebelliousness. One can see the reflections of the influence in the writings of BP Koirala or Parijat, whose poems and novels reflect existentialism and Marxism. Works of translation were very rare. Although the literary environment during those times was hopeful, the writings hardly reflected the voices of the marginalised.

Current environment

As publishers and newspapers proliferated and the constitution guaranteed press freedom, writings and translations reached a new height. Singh (2014) writes, "Bookshops like Mandala Book Point and Educational Book House ventured into publishing. Suvani Singh writes, "Nepa-laya conceptualised a revival of the Nepali language publishing industry, in every sense. They wanted not just a new look but also a new style of writing and a marketing strategy, unlike any other for a book." For example, Palpasa Café by Narayan Wagle broke records and set new trends.

We now have many publications focusing on different genres and missions. For example, Akshar Creations focuses on women's writings. Now one sees many publishing houses being established to publish books of literary genres, such as Fine Print, Phoenix Books, Shikha Publication, Book Hill and many others. Compared to the past, editorial processes and marketing strategies are gradually developing. Manuscripts are being reviewed and edited, the production values of books are of good quality, and promotional campaigns often accompany the launch of a book.

Compared to the past, the current literary writing is more open, decentralised and multivocal. For example, Rajan Mukaraung's Madan Prize winner Daminivir is what we might call in Mikhail Bakhtin's word "polyphonous", meaning the novel houses voices of the marginalised. The novel decentres the centre and the traditional form of writing fiction by introducing a movement called "srijansil arajakta", meaning "creative anarchy". Similarly, Bina Thing Tamang's collection of stories Yambuner, meaning "near Kathmandu", highlights the voices and lived experiences of the marginalised. Also, Amar Neupane's Seto Dharti, meaning "white earth", can be an epitome to reflect on the lived experiences of marginalised women that the younger generation of today needs to know. One can take many other works of fiction that speak the voices of the marginalised, such as Shyam Saha's Pather or Nayan Raj Pandey's Ular, or Krishna Abiral's Kariya or Saraswati Pratixya's Nathiya or Nilam Karki Niharika's Yogmaya.

Abhi Subedi writes, "Literature in Nepali in recent times is producing works that are written about the subaltern people and the ethnic power of aesthetics. This is a new development and is sure to bring new energy in Nepali literary writing. The total experience of writing in Nepal is related to this tremendous resurgence of voices and aesthetic perceptions and experimentations."

For the effectiveness of writing any genre, one can introduce unique techniques and tools, language and diction, and presentation and structure, rather than just experimentation for writing per se. And, yes, an audience should be in mind. For a wider readership of Nepali literature, writing in English about the marginalised and doing the best translations of the best Nepali writing about them is a must. Moreover, for Nepali literature to flourish, a healthy tripartite relationship of publishers, writers and critics seems significant. (**Published in The Kathmandu Post dated April 17, 2022**).

Education System In Need Of Change

WHAT WE ARE STILL PRACTICING in the academic institutions of Nepal is what Paulo Freire calls "the 'banking' concept of education," which means "education becomes an act of depositing, in which the students are the depositories, and the teacher is the depositors. Instead of communicating, the teacher issues communications and makes deposits which students patiently receive, memorise, and repeat. Mugging up everything that the teachers preach in class does not help one be a better citizen and a critical thinker.

Need of research

Although there are many academic institutions in Nepal, education practices are all about preaching and memorising, and repeating and rotting. Such activities are guided by the institutions' final exam point of view. Many classes are simply run devoid of a culture of research and learning, classroom discussions, and critical thinking. If such practices of merely memorising and learning continue to exist in Nepali classrooms, the future of the nation might be bleak.

Students usually have the impression that remembering what their teachers say can make them successful in their academic endeavours. However, the students fail to think of its adverse effect on their future career. This is either because of the fear of being beaten up by the teacher or of failing to receive good marks. Students continue to believe that each word the teacher uses in the classroom is like the ultimate truth. Neither the students want to go beyond what the teachers say in the classroom, nor do they wish to be critical of him. Thus, the students make their teachers, parents and themselves happy.

While lecturing in the classroom, the teacher should be able to deconstruct the myth and realise that the students are not there to be fed. S/he should also not feel that his/her knowledge is absolute, true, and unquestionable. The classroom culture in advanced countries helps students be critical. Most of the assignments in the classroom do not test their IQs, but their level of critical thinking and how they see the world outside the box. They are asked to read texts critically and think creatively and write, for example, a 10-page paper critically. They are asked to come to each class being prepared to discuss and present a different view and perspective, not just to deposit what the instructor said the other day.

Without making inquiries, reading critically and raising questions or making claims or arguments is not adequate. That kind of practice never gives an opportunity to everyone to be truly human. Freire writes, "Knowledge emerges only through invention and reinvention, through the restless, impatient, continuing, hopeful inquiry human beings pursue in the world, with the world, and with each other."

This minimises students' creative powers. They should be inspired to communicate.

We should opt for writing through mental process, research, outside study and observations. But we are hardly taught to look at the same piece or article from different vantage points and discuss. We are made to dance to the rhythm of the teachers' language. We are still accustomed to what Berlin writes in his article "Rhetoric and Ideology in the Writing Class"— the "authoritarian classroom, a place where the teacher holds all power and knowledge and the students is a receptacle into which information is poured, a classroom that is loveless, arrogant, hopeless, mistrustful and critical." We never become aware of the fact that the classroom is a place where students and teachers interact and share experiences within a social and interdisciplinary framework.

It is necessary for the teachers to teach the students to be creative, transformative, and dialogic. Teachers are required to teach students to read and write a summary of an essay, instead of writing a summary for them. Teachers must be able open a window of opportunity for students' discussion. They should bring out problems so that students try to solve them.

Drastic changes

It would not be an overstatement to say who we are, what we are doing, and where we are heading is the result of what we have learnt in the classroom. And most of politicians, policymakers, and academicians are the products of the same education system in Nepal. Until and unless we change the concept that a teacher knows everything and student knows nothing, we cannot bring about drastic changes in the education system. What we need today is the type of education that can upgrade our nation's image on the world stage. (***Published in the Rising Nepal dated April 10, 2022***)

Breaking Indoctrination Culture

MANY PEOPLE IN NEPAL support a party or its ideology not because they have a good grasp of it, but because of the impact from a culture of indoctrination that bolsters their unwillingness to alter their long-cherished beliefs in a party. This is how many people are motivated whether to support the party they have been supporting for a long time. A few like-minded Nepali people believe that associating oneself with a particular party is identifying one's moral obligation in the line of their predecessors.

Motivating factors

Regarding why one becomes a strong believer of a particular party is not always obvious. However, the believer's motivations are usually shaped by two factors: their sense of duty to the party and the ideology the party carries and a sort of fear to alter the party allegiance even after the ideology the party fails to carry. Many believers don't want to alter the status quo, the habit of supporting one party for a long time. This habit defines one's perception regarding the compliance or defiance with the party. One can observe this, not only in the context of a developing country like Nepal but also in the context of developed nation like the United States.

For example, the American Democratic Party was for over a hundred years the party of the poor White Southern man and the present Republican Party began life as an antislavery party. It was not until the 1960s that the Democratic Party lost favour in the southern United States because of its support of pro minority policies and the ideology of the Republican Party shifted towards a more White Anglo Saxon Protestant stance. Even when people disagree with party leadership, they often commit themselves to the party come hell or high water, and often seem to vote against their own interests for the sake of party. Parties capitalise on blind adherence by counting on certain sections of the populace to cast a vote for them as they have done for generations.

Ideology is a system of definite views, ideas, conceptions, and notions adhered to by some class or political party. A closer inspection of political ideologies reveals that they dominantly influence the perceptions of the commoners who mostly believe in a political party or the ideology it carries.

Mostly affected by the ideologies are the marginalised, the poor, the disabled, women, Dalits, untouchables, and those who do not have their own voices except for believing in the party ideology. The party ideologies are hegemonic, meaning they are coercive and overbearing in the minds of the marginalised.

Half of the Nepali population lives below the poverty line the majority being women. According to the 2021 census, about seven to eight per cent of the population has an assortment of disabilities, mostly situated in the "lower caste" population. Most of the politicians representing such demographics in parliament and bureaucracy are rich, male, "abled," and upper caste, even those including the politicians who represent the marginalised and the group of subalterns who, according to Gayatri Spivak, do not have their own narratives and voices.

This scenario creates a fissure between the politicians' perceptions of the marginalised and the marginalised people's perceptions of themselves. When politicians' ideology fails to address the perceptions of the marginalised, the agendas, policy designs, and constitution making process cannot reflect, address, and ameliorate their conditions, to be specific.

However, we continue to believe in those ideologies that we have been indoctrinated with in the hope that one day our conditions will be better. Even these days, the marginalised and disadvantaged populations are living in politicians' narratives believing in their ideology and obeying orders to go out in the street holding placards without any questions, without any knowledge of being the politicians' useful tools to garner their own interests but thinking that one day their lives would be improved.

Narratives

Thus, many of the adherents and believers of a party have been living through the narratives of politicians who can hardly represent the marginalised, but instead continue to mete out false ideologies to woo and canvas the poor for their own political gain. In their article "The role of ideology in politics and society," Kevin Harrison and Tony Boyd write that ideological assumptions thus affect all aspects of society: family, political parties and pressure groups, local and national politics, and international politics. One should know the ideologies closely to better understand how they are addressing the conditions of the marginalised.

Many people are enmeshed in such a political culture, and perhaps, due to lack of education that one holds fast to old beliefs even in the light of new thinking that demonstrates the errors of our way. They are unable to think outside of the box to realise how they view themselves and how political ideologies restrain or set them free.

It is time to rethink whether politicians are really executing public will, while bringing up their ideologies that, they say, are for ameliorating the conditions of the marginalised. It is vital to peruse whether we are merely the adherents of parties because our predecessors supported them. If we still cannot break our blind faith in particular parties and party ideologies that are outdated, we will never find our conditions improved, let alone the conditions of the marginalised. (Published in the Rising Nepal dated March 17, 2022)

Can a Man Cry?

———

"TODAY MY WIFE HURT me, Tulasi," a very close friend of mine told me in a lachrymose tone the other day. "My wife said, 'you are like a woman. Go marry a man. You should have not married me.'" Flabbergasted, I asked him what the cause of this outburst was. He looked very worried and upset. "She was mad at me for not having the manly qualities of strong and bold attitudes," he said. I wondered what he meant by not having manly qualities. He enlightened me further saying, "I was sick and feeling weak while suffering from cold fever and lying down on my bed. I didn't even have enough energy to show my manly trait. I was emotional then. I think that is probably the reason." I looked at him and wondered in a dilemma because I could not think of any advice that would lessen his grief and ease the pain he experienced in his relationship with his wife.

"I should have married someone whom I dated for a few months until I knew her better and understood what she would expect from her would be husband instead of choosing an arranged marriage, and my life would not be so complicated." He kept going on. "I must have made her unhappy because I am the one who she wants to change."

"You don't have to change. Just be you who you are," I told him. "Just try to understand her, that's it." However, I knew my advice was a little lacking for him. "Yes, I try to understand her. I go shopping with her. I tend to be okay with her about what she wants to buy or wear or whatever pleases her. I help her with her make-up and also wait for her with heavy stacks of dresses in both hands until she comes out from the fitting room," he said. "Although, I get frustrated, you know. Our parents never had to do that, nor did our mothers bother our fathers about all this nonsense. And still, she keeps talking baloney and making a song and dance. She asks me how she looks, and my answer does not make her happy. I am tired, dude." I realize he must have a modern wife who wants her husband to please her all the time, no matter how demanding she is, be a yes man about whatever decisions she makes outdoor and indoor, always be by her side, and make everything available that keeps her happy. "You are demanding, and you want me to please you like a woman needs to be pleased. You are a complete woman. That is what my wife said," my friend sounded desperate, putting his head in his hands, his body language showing that he is panicking. "Being a man, you cry about a little tiny thing, my wife says, how can I have feelings for you when I cannot see you as a man? It really is upsetting to me, that she thinks those things." He lights a cigarette and puffs in and puffs out. I suggest to him not to worry as everything would be alright. After he leaves, I think of him as being a close friend who is abandoned to despair.

In my parents' time, a man could be a man who hardly cried, no matter what struggles and trauma he had to go through. He had to make the family happy working outside and feeding them, but he never had time to spend with his wife while shopping or carrying her clothes while she tried them on in a fitting room. Washing clothes or doing laundry, cooking food or washing dishes, cleaning the kitchen and house or making the bed would be women's jobs; basically, not doing the work that a women was supposed to do made a man a man. A woman would do millions of things to please her husband; Hindu Literature from the *Kaamsutra* to *Swastani Bratakatha* interpreted women's duty and men's pleasure profoundly (These texts should not guide what should be the relationship between a husband and wife because times have changed and each being should be treated equally. I am myself against injustice and discrimination toward woman, but these days I am worried about some so-called modern women who want men to act like men and be their slaves when it pleases them. I apologize if I am being harsh here.)

Let me go back to my friend's situation. His wife wants him to act like a man. He should not cry even in pain because he is man. He should appear bold and strong all the time. At the same time, he should cook for her, clean the kitchen, keep everything neat and tidy, make more money, say "yes" to what she wants to do, never show he is bored or frustrated, or discouraged or lacks energy, join her shopping to carry her bargains when she tries them on in a fitting room and comes out preening every few minutes and expects him to say how wonderful she looks, help with her makeup, polishing her nails, bringing her a cup of tea in the morning, never complaining, never raising his voice at her, and be like a man. What a challenge my friend is coping with to attain this dream of real manhood!

Now times have changed. To be a man, one has to not only do what one had to do in my parents' time, but also has to do what a woman used to do at that time plus give them extra time and help. You can sweep the floor or clean the kitchen when it is dirty, cook the food when your wife is hungry, take her to some places for her pleasure, book a ticket for her to watch a night show, take her to a bar and give her a drink and dance with her or do whatever she wants you to do when you do not want to do, but never cry when you are in panic, when you are hurt, when you want to cry. Why? Because you are a man, you should not be a woman. At the last, a million-dollar question is: when can my friend cry like a woman when he needs to and still arouse feelings in her and be seen as a man?

Nothing Feels Like Home

"WHAT A PAINFUL LIFE living in a foreign land!" my roommate exclaimed. When I looked at him, he was listening to Deusi songs online and trying to feel the presence of the Tihar festival around him. I had never seen him listening to such Deusi songs, only English rap music before. "This was the song we used to play Deusi in," he said, also wishing me to listen to the song. At that moment, I realized that nobody could forget his root culture, no matter how much he is ingrained in foreign culture.

My roommate, who left Nepal six years ago, has been living in the US as a US citizen. He has missed Dashain and Bhaitika, Nepalese cultural festivals, every year since the time he came here. "When I remember Bhaitika, I cannot help crying," he said. I have missed Bhaitika for four years. My sister must have been putting Dhaka topies and garlands of marigolds in her list every year when she misses me." Emotional and sad, he said, "I am alone here, except for the remembrance of the great festival I used to celebrate with my family." He felt the presence of aroma coming from sellroties during Tihar. He imagined the candles and firecrackers illuminating the dark sky throughout the night. He remembered having fun by playing cards with his friends and relatives. Every house came to his mind where he used to go door to door to play deusi and bhailo with his friends. All of a sudden, he became so emotional that his eyes became teary. He could not control himself. "This is the first time in my life I cried," he said.

This is not only the situation of my roommate but the reality of every Nepali who has been living abroad. For many Nepali people, to be in the US is a matter of pride, but it is also a matter of pain because every year many Nepali like my roommate cry for the loss of what they had in their homeland, for the loss of their culture where they were born and brought up, and for the loss of the festivals they celebrated with their families. Like every year, this year also the Nepali people in the US pantomimed their pain and suffering through the dramatic enactment on the occasion of Dashain and Tihar. They manifested their anxiety, frustration, boredom, and obligation of being in the US and expressed how much they missed their culture and how painful it was to miss their culture. Notwithstanding the use of modern facilities they are living with in the US, they are unable to supplant the irreparable loss caused by a cultural gap or by missing the culture with abundant physical infrastructure they are living in. Those infrastructures have merely provided them with physical comfort but not mental, psychological, and emotional comfort.

This year too many Nepali like my roommate endeavored to mitigate the pain of missing the festivals, the part of culture, through songs or dramatic performances which are played and performed. They either listened to the songs or acted by themselves to relieve the emotional pain they had. They cried in pain and the tears washed their pain. This is how they brought mental purgation and emotional catharsis. It was a different way of fulfilling the urgent desire of being in the root culture and not missing the festival they celebrated in their homeland. It was because it would mitigate the instinctual, psychological, and mental urge to celebrate the festival with family. It was the manifestation of latent feeling as a result of being in a different geography with a different culture far away from the homeland.

Indeed, when we miss our culture, it becomes a sore that merely gives us emotional pain with no healing ointment. I also sobbed my heart out during Bhaitika. I did so because it could mitigate the pain I had for missing the tika from the hand of my sister. Let this year Tihar bring peace and prosperity in the nation so all Nepali people will not love to go abroad just to suffer the pain of missing festivals. (*Published in Myrepublica 2010*)

Message from Political cartoons

SOME ARE SPHINX LIKE — half man and half animal. Some are hairy like orangutans. Some look clownish — small body size but big head and big belly. Some look transgendered in their outfits, for example a male politician is dressed up in a Sari and blouse, the other in a T-shirt and mini skirt. These are political cartoons. Cartoons are funny and satirical. Wilfrid Wood says, "Wonderful-looking people can be boring as hell. Mouldy old potatoes can have a lot going for them."

One may witness such political cartoons on social media as they have been posted or shared by social media users or that have been printed in newspapers or published online. Some of them are sketched by cartoonists while others are made from animation or are replaced with memes. Such cartoons speak volumes about the politicians who should take something away from the cartoons. Such cartoons or memes aim to — more than entertain — mock, deride, look down upon and loathe politicians for their unaccountability and irresponsibility.

Long history

The use of political cartoons has a long history and it started with a purpose of satire. Brianna Vittachi writes, "Cartoonists started using satire to convey moral or political messages to the public as a means of entertainment, journalism, propaganda and nationalism." According to Haley Grant, "Benjamin Franklin's iconic "Join or Die" is acknowledged to this day as America's first official political cartoon." It portrays a severed snake whose divided parts represent the divided colonies. This cartoon emphasised, Grant writes, "the importance of unity and sparked a sense of nationality among the colonies that ultimately drove the fight for independence." By the early 20th century, the cartoons moved into animated moving images.

In Nepal, we have started noticing political cartoons more frequently after the restoration of democracy. With the abundance of social media, people have been frequently coming across such cartoons and sharing them. Sharing such political cartoons or memes by social media users reflect on people's psychology when it comes to the perception of politicians. When there is a gap between the politicians' words and deeds, it brings in hateful emotions amongst people that cartoonists and animators succeed to catch. Such cartoons pacify people's anger against the politicians.

The meanings of cartoons have expanded. Not only are they simply satirical, but also such cartoons become symbols and metaphors — as politicians being incapable, inhuman, and jokers — that represent people's ridiculed perceptions of Nepali politicians. Brianna Vittachi writes, "Cartoons commonly enlist symbolism, exaggeration, labelling, analogy and irony to rouse humour or skepticism in an audience." As the politicians fail to perform what they promised to accomplish in front of Nepali people and their role of leadership remains invisible, their political image crumbles like a castle made of cards.

When responsible politicians are not found working responsibly, cartoonists and animators start metamorphosing the former's real mugshots making them look funny, unrealistic, and shameful unlike Gregor Samsa, a character in Franza Kaflka's story "metamorphosis". One morning Samsa wakes up to find himself transformed into "monstrous vermin" which showcases the reality of a modern man burdened with numerous responsibilities.

Cartoons of Nepali politicians demonstrate different demeanors, for example, a Sphinx like mugshot display bestial nature of the character, a clownish look bring out concealed character who is just a butt of joke in the position he is in, a male character dressed up in a Sari and blouse reflect on the effeminate character of a male politician, perhaps to reflect on the character's dual nature, his lack of judgment, reasoning, and leadership quality, so to speak in the context of patriarchal/ chauvinistic culture.

Such images on social media show how capable cartoonists and animators are to grab Nepali people's perceptions and venting emotions against some politicians who have made many mistakes in the past and continue to repeat them, committing irresponsible deeds frequently and yet not realising it. Sharing such political cartoons on social media means losing trust upon the politicians and doubting their capability and capacity, making fun of them, and losing respect that the politicians could deserve if they remained accountable to people.

Proliferation

The proliferation of such political cartoons on social media gives those who are frustrated with politics and politicians a sense of satisfaction. The purpose of political cartoons is not only to entertain people projecting them looking funny and hilarious, but also making politicians more responsible and dutiful. Such cartoons are the punishments given to the politicians for their dirty politics, which is also the reflection of frustration, anxiety, and pessimism Nepali people are coping with during 'wait and see' the future of Nepal. Such cartoons, on one hand, relieve the mind of a frustrated Nepali, and morally obligate politicians to be responsible to what they are responsible for, on the other.

Hope Nepali politicians are fully aware of such cartoons proliferated in social media and learn a lesson and be informed about their duty and responsibility. The cartoons are, symbolically speaking, for politicians to take something positive away from and bring about some positive change in the leadership more than for people to look and laugh at and share on social media. (***Published in The Rising Nepal dated August 8, 2022***)

Open The Window for Opportunity

—

ON 25TH OF APRIL, 2015 around 12 P.M., an earthquake with a magnitude of 7.9 on the Richter scale hit Nepal killing and severely injuring more than 9000 and 19000 people respectively. It triggered an avalanche on the tallest mountain of the world that cost around two dozens of human lives and other deadly avalanches that disfigured the Himalayas. The earthquake flattened entire villages and demolished and destroyed centuries old world heritage sites in Kathmandu, Patan, and Bhaktapur Darbar Square. A historic tower, Dharahara collapsed into a pile of rubble. Major aftershocks furthered the devastation, not only destroying everything, but also inculcating fear and trauma in the minds of many people. The quake abandoned them to despair. Similarly, in 2020, Covid-19 pandemic terrified the world costing the lives of millions by now. Not only are these two examples, but also are there many other examples in the past which show that such natural disasters and pandemics have been existing phenomenon since time immemorial and will continue to happen in the future. In the book "History of the World Map by Map," the author mentions that such natural disasters and pandemic are inevitable to occur.

No science can overcome nature and pandemic right away. Nor are such calamities scheduled to occur, nor does one know how long they would stay, and when they would leave. If someone knew such things ahead of time, they could prevent people from dying in numbers, for example, if one had predicted the earthquake could hit Nepal exactly on the same date ahead of time, Nepali people would not have to suffer the loss as much as what they witnessed seven years ago today.

Earthquakes are not new to Nepal that had suffered from other major earthquakes in the past, such as the major earthquake in 1934, and other quakes and tremors that followed. Geologist also have declared Nepal as one of the earthquake prone nations. If one studies the geology of Nepal, one sees that quakes take place when tectonic stress builds up in the plates of the earth. The earthquake in 1934 in Nepal was also caused by this natural tectonic stress. Nepal is sandwiched between two boulder like nations China and India, where the Indian plates under-thrusts the Eurasian plates occupying the central section of the Himalayan arc, geologists say.

Costlier Calamities

We also experienced that the aftermath after such calamities was even worse, especially in developing countries like Nepal, when the government fails to address it properly and adequately. We saw support coming from various nations during such difficult times. When a natural disaster hits any nation, aid and support from various places is inevitable and important, no matter how well equipped the country is. When the country has not enough resources, it is unthinkable that the country will survive on its own without aid and support from national and international agencies and governments. In the case of Nepal, we have seen the prevalence of deep humanity, love, and kindness that everyone has shown nationally and internationally, through agencies, charity organizations, and institutions. National armies who make the call and public servants that volunteer have shown heroic deeds risking their lives in rescue and relief operations for the victims in times of crisis like this. However, when the government becomes more cautious about the future possibilities of such calamities and prepare for them in advance, such catastrophes wouldn't be costlier, and humanitarian works would be quicker while saving the lives of many people.

Since natural calamities and pandemics are unavoidable, what government and the people in policymaking, and interested stakeholders can do is to analyze the future possibilities of them and prepare accordingly so they don't have to witness the irreparable loss of lives and many other valuable things. By now, we have learned how the lack of proper preparation for future calamities turned out to be costlier financially, emotionally, and psychologically.

Window for Opportunity

Learning the lesson from the past is crucial. Such crises in the nation must be realized as the window for opportunity to design and enact policies for crisis management and to address any future possible natural calamities and pandemics. Policymakers, interested stakeholders, and people affected by the incidents should be able to come up with new agendas to address such disasters in the future. In the developed nations, for example America, they always take the crisis and pandemic as the window for opportunities to design and enact policies to address the future possible national crisis of the similar nature they witness. Thus, such crises need to be discussed as issues for future policy agendas. For example, if we are thinking of the future policies and the agendas regarding future possible earthquake damages, one can think of proper agendas in policy making related to different issues, such as management crisis, earthquake policies, building the houses, the location of the construction and so on.

In this matter, media also should play a significant role.

The agenda media brings in should be more researched based, facts, evidence that include public participations, communications, various interest groups, to make the agendas democratic and viable. Learning from the past, it is high time to discuss such topics and formulate crucial policies accordingly so when such calamities occur in the future, like earthquake or any pandemic, one will not witness big loss. If the policymakers do not take the crisis as the window for opportunities, it will be closed and the chance to take the opportunities will be no longer possible. In his book "Agendas, Alternatives, and Public Voices,"

John W. Kington writes that Policy window is a scenario in which the ground is fertile for the uptake of an idea that has been proposed for a long time but never implemented, but it has found its time that one needs to catch. So, let's take such catastrophes and pandemics as the windows of opportunities to form policies and address future possible crises.

Enlightened life

ONE DAY I RAN INTO a Caucasian lady in her early twenties as I was roaming around in Atlanta downtown. Her fair skin was concealed by artistically designed tattoos that, at first, gave me an impression of her embroidered clothes. I wondered and asked why such tattoos that blanketed her body. She smiled wryly and said, "My choice, something different, just trying to celebrate my life!" At first, I was flustered by her answer. I couldn't acknowledge the number of tattoos when I imagined myself in her shoes. My little brain of around three pounds wrestled to understand her perception of life.

"Man's release from his self-incurred tutelage," a French Philosopher and social theorist Michael Foucault said about enlightenment. What he meant was being tutored or having to undergo tutelage is man's inability to make use of his own reason without direction from another. According to him, to have the courage to use one's own reason is what, Foucault suggests, we call enlightenment. Slowly, without being convinced, I come to a point to agree that she must have used her self-knowledge, the knowledge released from her self-incurred tutelage, not being fettered from social normative values. Perhaps, she was living an enlightened life in her own way.

These days I see many young people practicing self-incurred tutelage—sometimes youngsters, rappers, celebrities, and, at times, even so-called philosophers. The so called "self-incurred tutelage" does not limit itself to making tattoos on their bodies only, but doing some "deviant" things, such as smoking Marijuana, boozing, and others leading to criminal, prurient, and suicidal activities.

We have seen many Hollywood celebrities dying of drug overdoses. For example, renowned and revered pop singer Michael Jackson died of drug overdose and the simultaneous use of poly substance, a combination of propofol and benzodiazepines. Marilyn Monroe who was (and still) known for her blonde beauty, also remained as a pop and cultural icon, died of a drug overdose. Sunny Leone who was born in a rich family and also was an educated and business woman turned herself into a porn star. An American country singer Mindy McCready shot herself to death. These incidents are the outcomes of their choices, the reasons of the celebration of their lives, perhaps being released from "self-incurred tutelage." But I doubt. Is this the release from their self-incurred tutelage? Perhaps the self-reasons they used to debunk the normative society that, they felt, chained them.

What if we start living our life completely different from socially accepted norms? Does this kind of freedom of choice coming from "self-incurred tutelage" add any value to human life, to the idea of enlightenment, to a democratic society?

A few days ago, my wife opined that "Life is not just all about living, it's about not losing hope to live it lively." In the wake of her status, I contemplated what life really is. A hermit might be happy living in a cave with serpents slithering around him, can live a celibate life and abandon social pleasure. On the other hand, a hedonist devotes his life to the pursuit of pleasure and self-gratification. Perhaps each of them has their own definition of life inspired by "self-incurred tutelage."

These two but opposite versions of life's philosophy— one coming from "self-incurred tutelage" and another coming from social normative knowledge— create a dialectical tension on how life really should be celebrated: or what is right and what is wrong? Is life about living the way one wants to live, or just to live, or to live with lively hope? Questions multiply.

When we mull over these questions, the definition of life doesn't stop to the point where we define life as merely a life that requires certain things to prove it is living. Life perhaps more than a tree grows, or its branches spread, or the leaves sprout or the colors change. If we don't look for certain things and other creative resources of our lives within ourselves, life is boring, and it may divert us towards deviant things.

In his poem "Dream Songs," John Berryman writes:

Life, friends, is boring

we must not say so.

After all, the sky flashes,

the great sea yearns,

we ourselves flash and yearn,

and moreover, my mother told me as a boy

(repeating) "Ever to confess you're bored

means you have no inner Resources."

Is life boring so people use their self-incurred knowledge to do such things that the normative society considers deviant to enliven their boring life? Or are they confessing their boring lives through arts, songs, poems, drugs, death, and destruction and other criminal and suicidal activities? Does it mean those people who destroy their lives coming from their own choices released from self-incurred "tutelage"? Is that the enlightenment as how Foucault might be defining? Won't such practices change the meaning of what it means to live with hope and to live life lively? Thus, keeping our "self-incurred" tutelage in check and balance through the lens of our normative society might be the real beauty of living an enlightened life, rather than letting our lives flow without any horse-bridal. (2022 AD)

Comparing Cultures That Belittle Women

IN HER ESSAY, "ONCE upon a Quinceanera," Julia Alvarez quotes what a girl says when asked why not give boys a quinceanera, "Boys do not need a quinceanera. Boys are born men but girls turn into women." The phrase "turns into women" indicates how the society views women differently as if they are "made to be" objects. Quinceanera is a female coming-of-age tradition known among Hispanic communities when a female turns fifteen. In this rite of passage, they throw a lavish party—what they say is "throw the house out of the window"— to celebrate and also manifest her newly arrived sexuality. It prepares her to get married and have babies, silently indicating that "a girl disappeared forever inside a woman." The tradition dictates that the young girl is crowned with a tiara which symbolizes her sense of self-confidence. Indirectly, this tradition is preparing them to receive male attention, which directly or indirectly objectify them, that goes without a notice in the culture. Alvarez writes citing an interviewee's view "the quinceneara is the sanctioned way that a nice family says, okay, now, my daughter may receive male attention."

While talking about "quinceneara," it is logical here to introduce Chhaupadi, a conservative Nepali coming-of-age tradition which is still practiced in some nooks and crannies of the western region in Nepal. Both cultures "quinceneara" and "Chhaupadi" in two different geographical locations can be somewhat comparable in a different way. Chhaupadi is a tradition in which a girl is kept in a dark shed during her first period to prevent her from seeing the view outside or the light, from being in touch with men while at the same time it is very symbolic to represent her coming of age toward her sexuality, biological growth, and turning of a girl into a woman. In other words, she is symbolically ready for marriage and babies. Thus, both traditions have something in common— indicating their emerging sexuality and preparing them for womanhood.

Despite the symbolic similarities between two cultures, the difference is quinceanera is a lavish celebration thrown out there in public openly with food, fun, and fair, whereas chhaupadi is more conservative and superstitious, strongly patriarchal, and directly oppressive against women. The "Quinceanera" is regarded as "having become a deity, a culture heroine, the link between past and present, and the chhaupadi humiliates, disparages, and obliges women to think what they are undergoing is right and should be followed as their moral obligation.

Whatever maybe the differences or similarities, both are still restricting women from exercising their free will and independent performance. "All the girls admit that once they start developing, their parents, especially they call their parents papis, were like, Who are you going out with? Who was that that just called? Whose parents will be there?" Alvarez writes. Even after "a girl turns into a woman," there is still a male's restriction on the female and her body. Watching the quinceanera ceremony, Alvarez writes "I feel as if I have wandered into the back room where the femaleness of the next generation of Latinas is being manufactured, displayed, and sold." Looking at the culture in a deeper level, it is not empowering women, but rather turning them into a kind of commodity ready to be sold in the market.

Leaving the women who are advocates of feminism, or females like Alvarez who never had a quinceneara for herself besides, many girls who participate or are obliged to participate in a coming-of-age tradition, whether it is a quinceanera, or Sweet Sixteen, or Chhaupadi, seem to be not empowering women, and chhaupadi is even worsening those women's conditions who have been living in the remote areas of Nepal. Such cultures cannot make "her passage into womanhood quite successfull," but merely prepare them toward sexuality and restrict their bodies through males' control. Commenting on quinceanera, Alvarez writes it is an enactment of "fantasy." Alvarez further writes that "Quinceanera is like a rehearsal wedding without a groom," (which can also be compared somehow to Bell marriage in Newari community in Nepal), and "it is no wonder that girls end up getting pregnant soon after celebrating their quinces."

Although quinceanera seems to turn girls into women, empowering them and instilling a sense of self-esteem in them, it, indirectly, is interfering with women's mental, psychological, social, sexual, and cultural growth and making them vulnerable in their personal lives, whereas Chhaupadi is doing even directly, i.e. directly interfering with their lives and unalienable rights. Quinceanera makes teens to feel like the princesses momentarily by involving parents in profligacy, where as Chhaupadi directly makes the women of first time menstruation victims and feel humiliated, disgraced, and their lives being jeopardized. In that sense, Chhaupadi is directly worsening the conditions of Nepali women. It is always imperative to learn our cultures in light of other cultures to study the intensity of interference of the tradition with women's lives in women's cultural, social, psychological, and biological development.

Finally, we still have people like Alvarez who is very critical of the cultur,e such as quinceanera even if it seems to be way far more ameliorative than Chhaupadi. It is time for us to be critical of the cultures like Chhaupadi and revise it considering other traditions that empowers women rather than worsens their conditions. Cultures are bedrocks of our society so good cultures make our society a better place to live in. In the essay, Alvarez concludes, "Our cultural habits and traditions can be revised to work better for us in the new realities we are facing right now."

Living By Memories

THE OTHER DAY MY FATHER sent me a picture that I had not seen for the last twenty years, and it was a picture of myself kneeling on one knee, my favorite childhood pose in front of the photographer. My uncle had taken that picture. It took me a while to feel myself in the picture.

A young boy of ten is trying to maintain a cool photogenic face, putting on a smile, looking perhaps at the camera. His smile is very innocent. Eyes are wide open. His hairstyle is of the day, well combed and swept to one side, the very popular style of his age group perhaps. He loved mimicry just for the sake of mimicry. His mood in the picture reminds me of how he thinks of himself as the center of the universe.

A bright boy is relaxed and stress-free in the picture. He wears a full sleeve green dotted white shirt, which looks a way bigger than his bodily size, and black jeans pants, in vogue at his time, which his father had purchased after the boy's long hue and cry that all the other boys had jeans like these. The old worn-out belt looks as if it is squeezing all his trousers of 30 inches breadth around to fit his twenty-inch waist. The poor boy in the picture thinks of himself as fashionable, more handsome, and a man of the moment.

I touch the boy in the picture that has become slightly faded now and feel with it the memories of twenty years back. Nostalgia fills in my memories. I lost that boy in me. The innocence of the smile, the joy of mimicry, the benefits of making a hue and cry, and the freedom of the carefree life! All have vanished. I have lost the streets I walked along and the friends and foes I made on my way through life.

Like the fallen leaves of a tree, I left some players and characters of my life unconditionally. The future the young boy dreamed of has quickly become the past, and the days of those smiles are left behind. The too big longed for clothes made the boy feel so proud that sunny days have vanished in the blink of an eye.

Living in America for a decade or so and looking into the past, I do not want to live the present life. I want to go back to the time when I could live a frolicking life. I could jump into the rivulets carefree and come out soaked and exhausted.

I could play with bleating goats, waddling ducks, and could watch chickens pecking on tiny bits of gravel in the courtyard. I could enjoy seeing the butterflies fluttering across my head, farmers tilling the earth and planting crops. I could pick marigolds and daffodils and smell their fragrance; I could enjoy the sound of rain on the corrugated iron roof and water leaking from the roof of my countryside house in the rainy season.

Driving a car in America does not please me now. Enjoying the skyscrapers makes me say "wow," but does not emotionally appeal to me. The six to eight-lane highway in the US and the air-conditioned house give me physical comfort but never provide me with mental, emotional, and psychological tranquility.

Childhood life is the most precious life we ever lived. Life of innocence is always precious and momentous, and we realize its importance after we lose that innocence. As most of us live a hectic life after we gain maturity, we have hardly time to think of those precious moments of life. Life of innocence is very rapturous and that gets wrapped up as we enter a life of experience.

If my father had not sent that picture, I would have never become aware of that part of life, the life of innocence. The emotional part of human life is very essential to feed human thoughts, feelings, and human sentiment, to boost them, to enliven them, to invigorate life. After we grow up, we all become the slaves of our own experience and we do not have enough time to think of the essential sentimental and emotional aspects of human life that we had left behind when we were very young. Emotional aspects of human life come through his/her innocence by which our past survives.

That is why the British poet William Blake writes both poems, one on a "Lamb" and the other one on a "Tyger" to reflect on the two psychological aspects of human beings, that of innocence and experience. The lamb /childlike side of a human being is always important to reawaken and cherish the tiger/adult side of human beings; thus, both play an important role in human lives.

The photograph my father emailed me brought back the lamb side of me and my life through memories that are always cherished. Cherishing memories we can live a better life. Our life is always incomplete as we are leaving something behind before we are fully able to utilize it. However, it has its pleasure as we enjoy it without knowing it. By the time we know and analyze, we will, again, have already left that behind.

The ten-year-old boy in the picture, who is no one but myself, has right now made me very emotional and made me go back to that time. Living in the US and looking at the picture, the memories drawn out of the picture have pulled the strings of my heart. At this moment, I cannot go back except for living through memories, enjoying the moments of the past and cherishing them.

I have seen that many immigrant writers have lived through memories. Jhumpa Lahiri aches for the past and the memories. Similarly, Michael Ondaatje's "Running in the Family" is about cherishing the memories of seeing his own identity in those memories. No matter where one lives or migrates, one's heart is always for his root where he lived his past and childhood. That is why Salman Rushdie mentions in his book "Imaginary Homeland" something like this.

Oh, my shoes are Japanese,

Those trousers are English

Those hats are Russians

However, my heart is Indian.

Right now, my heart is very Nepali and more to the life of a boy in that picture in that photographic pose. We all live by memories! (***Published in in the Rising Nepal 21 Jan, 2022***)

Accept the Criticisms

GOVERNMENT NEEDS TO understand that appreciation of different perspectives and criticisms can only help the government become more accountable

I wonder why we are so critical of the government and the government is intolerant of criticisms that come from people. Who are critical of the government? They are people whose lives are still in lurch and whose aspirations are still not addressed. They are the media that carry the voices of such people.

When they become critical of the government, the government loses tolerance. So, we have Media Council Bill or rhetorical attacks our Prime Minister KP Oli launched against editors for not possessing a "strong heart" to praise the "good deeds." This has created a rift, or a lack of harmony between the Oli-led government and people or media that are critical of the government.

The majority government is unable to establish harmony with people due to "cheap talk" of the Prime Minister who never accomplishes what he promises on time, thus widening the gap between the government's roles and the people's expectations. So many of us profusely vent irrational feelings of dislike and hatred on social media toward the government that vows for the development of the country, but things are not happening in a way they are expected to. However, the government is not willing to accept this truth.

People are told to accept that development is happening. People consider that a lie because they think that just cutting ribbons or inaugurating some developmental projects will not lead the nation to prosperity. It is because livelihood of majority of Nepali people has not improved. Even today, according to Asian Development Bank, 26 percent of the population lives under the poverty line, and 34 out of 1000 babies born in Nepal die. Compared to global scenario, the conditions of many Nepali people are worse in terms of health, education, employment, and other facilities.

This gap between lack of delivery and people's expectations, the gap between the criticism and the government's lack of tolerance, the gap between the government's rhetoric/argument and people's observations/counterargument has created animosity and hatred against each other, between the majority government and people who have been waiting for too long for minimum change in life.

The government thinks that people and media, that are supposed to represent different voices of people from the streets, are biased against the government while the people and media realize that the government has been very slow in executing development projects effectively and efficiently. People think that it is all because of weak leadership, poor vision and "cheap talk." The more hesitant and obdurate the government becomes to listen to the media and people, the more the government will be lambasted upon. There will remain only a handful of loyalists to worship the government and the rest will be its critics.

The government expects each of us to trust it. Those who don't, according to Prime Minister Oli, are "regressive." Oli is biased toward those who do not like his talk. This is an indirect way of oppression of the critical voices. Oli tends to exclude people who are critical of the government, thus creating a further gap between the ruler and the ruled, discouraging people to equally participate with the government, and dismissing people who are critical of the government.

Oli-government should appreciate the criticisms as voices for reform. Otherwise, the government may feel humiliated and try to put more power and oppression upon people and media.

Those in the authority do not accept the criticism easily. Our education system tends to discourage criticism. For example, if a teacher is asked a question or argued against his/her views or performance by a student, s/he will feel more threatened and challenged. This way students' creativity, alternative thoughts, or out of the box perspective is squashed. This reflects in politics too. We are preached and supposed to follow or listen without questioning the practice or the views in politics, bureaucracy, and institutions. Thus, people who are given authority feel threatened or challenged when they are asked questions.

People in power start looking for a weapon to fight against such criticisms so that they can portray themselves as good leaders doing great things for the country. They aim at increasing the number of party loyalists by creating rhetoric that blames people who are critical of the government and appreciate those who praise the government. When people become 'yes' men it will create a hierarchy between the governor and the governed. Such gaps may kill the democratic practices and it may become detrimental to our development process.

The government needs to understand that appreciation of different perspectives and criticisms can only help the government become more accountable. The government needs to build positive attitude toward people who are critical of the government. The attitude that whatever the government is doing is flawless, bigger, better, and unquestionable will further create a rift between the government and the people and media who are critical of the government. Then the government tends to become autocratic as well. Criticisms help the government to diagnose its mistakes, which when rectified, can make people happy. (***Published in my Republica February 29, 2020***)

Back To Village: Away from City Cacophony

DILAPIDATED VEHICLES queue up in the traffic jam on the street in the valley. They emit black fumes, leaving its wispy trail behind where lies the weary building of the royal palace turned into a museum after the country abolished the monarchy on 28 May 2008. I struggle to muffle my mouth, and question, "why did I leave my village that gave me plenty of fresh air to breathe?" When the congestion becomes not only of vehicles but also of unwanted noise, carbon monoxide, traffic rule breakers, and political imbroglio, I vent my frustration at myself, "why the heck did I leave the peace of the countryside where I spent my childhood and adolescence?"

When I wake up to a cacophony of Kathmandu, I miss those days in the village when birds chirped on bamboo trees early in the morning, giving me a wake-up call. Bagmati River, which flows as if forlorn and gutter-filled, reminds me of how much I have missed the susurration of the Ramchandre river, clean and precinct—that now has become a relic of the past, that I can relish in my imagination. I can jump, whether dressed or undressed, into the river of my fantasy and swim. Nowhere do I find the joy in the valley these days.

Lure Of Town

Why did I sell and leave our four acres of land we owned and limit myself to the area of four aana in Kathmandu? Why did I sell the freedom I had in the village? What joy would I have when I brag about my house in Kathmandu? All these questions have now started ringing in my ears like an uninterrupted bell, forcing me to sell the property in the valley, go back to the village, and reinvigorate myself and feel like a Phoenix that could rise from its ashes.

Here in Kathmandu, everything feels morbid. Life is in a rush. There is no rhythm. The river I want to jump into carries gutter life. The road I want to travel to suffers from potholes, traffic jams, or black fumes. The people seem to be mechanical or melancholic. Politics is absurd. Politicians sit in for protest, polluting the daily chores of life. They spread illusions of patriotism and bring innocent lives from the countryside to Kathmandu for protests, distributing false dreams. They don't trust their government, nor the judiciary system. Power, pennies, and promiscuousness are what tend to be guidi ng principles of politicians' behaviour and attitudes. It becomes suffocating. I belch all the acids Kathmandu gives me and that mingles with the dust and fume in the air in the valley.

I enter a coffee shop just for a break for myself and contemplate Kathmandu over sips of coffee. Kathmandu remained an exotic place for many visitors and foreigners for years, for example, Pico Lyer in his book "Video Night in Kathmandu" describes his impression of Kathmandu in the 1980s as "delirious." He writes, "I felt as if I had tumbled into the jangled and kaleidoscoped subconscious of an opium freak." His description of Kathmandu is so "cool." In his description, he brings so many social, cultural, and religious paraphernalia into play. He portrays Kathmandu as "the land of mystic delights." Peter J, Karthik explores then Kathmandu even more picturesquely in his recent novel "Kathmandruids: Monomyths and many myths."

When I came to Kathmandu, I didn't think of these. I don't know how foreigners view Kathmandu these days, but in my heart, it always remained as a city of temples, the capital city of Nepal. When I came here, I only thought of my future and my career, my further studies, and going abroad. I only thought of Kathmandu as the biggest city of Nepal where we have big universities, big institutions, big airports, celebrities, politicians, and opportunities.

Deploring State

I never thought of the current deploring state of Kathmandu that has still failed to equally mete out the opportunities across the country even after the collapse of so many political systems and regimes that range from the Rana regime to the loss of monarchy to federal democratic republic. I never thought that the countryside joy I inherited within me would be sucked out of me by the suffocation of Kathmandu. I only chased my dreams that I thought Kathmandu would provide, but never realized how much I would miss the actual dream I would eventually vie for. Kathmandu has made many hearts that have come from villages seeking the opportunity weary. So much has happened, but that remains like "much ado about nothing."

I come out to the road in the evening and see women in their mid-twenties and mid-thirties selling ready-made Chinese cheap clothes on the street while breastfeeding their babies while black fumes still coming from the vehicles seem to adulterate the mother's milk. Men and women — their faces wrinkled like creases of a pair of trousers that were never ironed; they are supposed to be living a retired life now— are barbecuing corn on the wood-fire and selling them, and the customers still bargaining for the price. Some of the "Indian looking" Madheshi people selling chatpate are asking if I would want it while I see others eating and their tongues producing hot-spicy sounds that make the saliva roll down inside my mouth.

Chasing Dreams

I think all of them are chasing dreams, that could be bigger or smaller depending upon who views it in what way. There are many theories about dreams, but dreams are perceptions too, and they are matters of time, I reckon. What I once thought as my dream is not a dream anymore. Now I find my dreams in the valley becoming hazier, wandering like the smog that seems to cover the hills of the valley on the horizon. The village I left in search of my dream becomes my dream, taller and clearer.

In the village, I find peace, hard-working people on the farm, and organic life and vegetation. In the village, I will be the first to see the sun, the moon, and the stars. In the village, I can grow vegetables, fruits, and plants in the soil, can sweat and take a shower from tube water—bucket by bucket. In the village, I can dance to the rhythm of the plant leaves' twirling, can behold the sunset on the horizon, can listen to the moo-moo, or mew, or cock-a-doodle-do. In the village, I can be the king of my own life. Living in the Kathmandu valley, I have been missing all of them.

My dream is to grow rice and lentils on my farm and consume them as my meal. Who doesn't know about them? Whoever comes to visit Nepal does not go unaware of rice and lentils. Otherwise, ask Rory Stewart who wrote in his New York Times bestseller nonfiction "The Places in Between" – "I ate... rice and lentils, some nights adding black millet bread," that was the only food we ate once upon a time when my parents were very poor.

Let's make "back to the village" a reality, not just a dream! (***Published in the Rising Nepal 30 Apr, 2021***)

Politics of Impression

WHAT WE FAIL TO UNDERSTAND is most of the decisions we make come from our impressions, not from observations, computations, and contemplation, and they affect our judgment, evaluation, and the kind of initiatives we take, whether that be in politics or policymaking or in any citizenry participation. We lack mental effort.

Without mental effort, the ideas we come up with, the perspectives we have, the way we see the world, and the arguments we make to persuade others mostly come from our impressions. If we do not bother with testing and validating the impressions we have, our way of seeing the world might turn out to be incorrect. We usually have the habit of taking things for granted without testing our impressions or questioning them.

In his book "Thinking Fast and Slow," Daniel Kahneman writes about two systems that work in human mind: System 1: "it operates automatically and quickly, with little or no effort and no sense of volunteer control" (p.20). System 2: "It allocates attention to the effortful mental activities that demand it, including complex computations. The operations of System 2 are often associated with the subjective experience of agency, choice, and concentration" (p.21). In this regard, we can also relate System 1 and System 2 to the two psychological forces of human psyche, i.e., impressions and reasoning. Impression is very quick to react while reasoning slows it down.

Going back to the idea of impressions, System 1 is a lot closer to immediate impressions based on how we respond to the ideas or objects or the world, thinking without effort. However, System 2 demands slow thinking and concentration. We can make a connection between these systems. We are accustomed to the culture of blaming each other and bickering, forming opinions and judgments for and against the opposition parties or political leaders.

Biased perceptions

We blame others so quickly without a second thought. For example, we quickly, without even thinking of or contemplating or computing it, call someone an "agent of RAW" if he/she talks in a favor of India or "Rajabadi," the King's person if it is in a favor of the King or so. We say so because of the kind of immediate impressions we have, but that's not always right. We make the similar intuitive judgments about women, Dalits, and the marginalized and biasedly represent them in politics and policymaking. Based on our biased perceptions of them, we make judgments on them. Therefore, we have lost the process of slow thinking that demands research, observations, facts, computations, and findings.

Sometimes what we speak from our impressions is correct, but not always. It is because some impressions come from our habits, familiarity, and everyday experience. We can immediately say two plus two is four, but we need to dilate our pupils to start thinking and computing slowly when we are asked what the outcome is when 36 is multiplied by 49. We have lost the art of mathematical computation before passing judgment on someone if we are merely relying on the impressions we have.

In our social, political, and cultural sphere, we are so quick to blame, predict, decide, and conclude just merely based on the impressions, and perhaps prejudices, personal interests, and superstitious beliefs. We fail to understand the consequences of fast thinking based on impressions. In politics, it is much easier and far more enjoyable to identify and label the mistakes of others than to recognize our own because we form the statements from the impressions and do not cultivate the habits of listening to informed opinions of others. Without slow thinking, we fail to diagnose our own biased intuitive impressions and, therefore, cannot improve the ability to identify and understand errors of judgment and choice, in others and eventually in ourselves.

Sometimes, we tend to believe in what the majority says. Or we might have gotten the impressions from topics and issues published and discussed in the mainstream media, and we associate ideas. Based on them, we form our opinions that populate our mind. However, we might have failed to reach the root cause of the issues or see things outside the box. Thus, serious issues might have slipped away from our awareness. Our own thinking might be imprisoned by our cognitive biases. Sometimes we are swept away by emotions, overconfidence that are formed based on our impressions. We always look for easy answers without contemplating and computing it. Thus, thinking slow is very important. Thinking slow, according to Kahneman, is the process of mental work: "deliberate, effortful, and orderly" (p.20).

Ego

Statements, ideas, judgments, and decisions from impressions are illusory. Thus, we must learn to mistrust our impressions, learn to be suspicious of our own feelings. For all of this needs a slow thinking. Slow thinking demands dilation of the pupils of the eyes. Psychologist Eckhard Hess describes the pupil of the eyes as "a window to the soul." Slow thinking is a removal of mental ego, and a try to understand others' informed perspectives, taking everyone's' ideas into considerations. Whether that be in politics or policymaking or in any citizenry participation, we all need to utilize both System 1 and System 2 to check and balance one another. There should be the practice of mental effort. Instead of blaming or judging others, one should think of correcting oneself.

Thus, the politics of impressions must be corrected through System 2, and mental efforts must be utilized whether that be in politics or policymaking or as a conscious citizen of the nation. (***Published in The Rising Nepal 28 Oct, 2021***)

Cultural Understanding of Gender to Assess the Cases of Sex and Rape

ON THE 1st of October 2019, Krishna Bahadur Mahara, the then speaker of Nepal's lower house of parliament, resigned as he was accused of raping a woman who worked in his office. The court has exonerated him on the 16th of February 2020. This scenario propelled me to proffer something on cultural understanding of gender to assess the cases of sex and rape.

In this article, I want to underscore how gender and gender roles are defined and discussed in the context of Nepal. When they are not discussed as much as they need to be in many forms and forums, such as media, schools, communities across different nooks and crannies of the country, the society always lags behind. On top of that, if the society is patriarchal, women suffer more by being exposed to vulnerability and volatility—resulting, for example, into the cases of rapes and sexual assaults as we have seen women being suffered in many occasions, for instances. Failing to understand culture that defines gender roles, we tend to discriminate against women.

We have been hearing sad news that have been reported on many occasions, not only by Nepali media, but also by international media—for example, about a young woman being bitten by a snake in an abandoned shade where she has to spend days and nights during her period (The New York Times report entitled "Shunned During Her Period, Nepali Woman Dies of Snakebite" published on July 9, 2017). Even The Rising Nepal, the most leading English daily newspaper of the state has reported many cases and stories on gender and sexual violence. The incidents are innumerable, such as about a young girl whom a guy sprinkles acid on her face for refusing his marriage proposal, about another young girl who is gang raped, about a child who is molested by her own father.

Although The Rising Nepal has reported on unreported sexual violence on boys entitled "Sexual Violence against Boys Remains Unreported" dated 24th December 2019, in patriarchal society, the case of sexual violence on women surpass. Usually, the victimized female is liable to bear all the blame for her being assaulted because she couldn't be "moral" and "fully-covered" that tantalized men to act upon their bodies. Thus, in patriarchal society, cultural understanding of gender is very important in the context of Nepal to understand the cases of rape. We will understand sex and gender more if you understand our culture that defines gender in terms of gender roles and other dos and don'ts. This will help us better understand the cases of rapes or other social problems associated with it.

In the context of Nepal, sex has been deemed as taboo and gender has still been narrowly defined, only through the lens of either male or female. Thus, Nepali society still finds it hard to accept how there does exist other sexes including transgendered and transvestites beyond the heteronormative idea of male and female. In such societies, people of other gender are prone to be more vulnerable. Until we look at the cultural practices that define gender roles out of the box, policies alone won't ameliorate the conditions of men and women, meaning gender roles that have been assigned to both men and women have oppressed men as well because they hesitate to challenge the normative practices of a society. Until or unless there is proper education on sex, rape, sexuality, and gender to be introduced and be discussed in many levels— that be academic or policy, sex and gender— discrimination continues to take place and rape cases continue to occur.

Similarly, another problem that persists in terms of sex and gender is not to discuss such topics and to consider them as less important than the topics of politics. Such practices continue legitimizing and institutionalizing sex and rape as taboo and gender discriminations. This creates the culture where the rape becomes permitted and permeable.

Although we have seen Nepali society has advanced compared to the past, when it comes to the discussion of sex and gender, the topic is knowingly or unknowingly belittled. Our policies and education are examples that discuss sex only in terms of health and marriage, not in terms of desire and human needs. Most of our policies or education seem to be founded on the ground of patriarchal ethos that validate male over female, male's sexual prowess over female's "hysterical" body, resulting into the cases of vulnerability of women and people of sexual orientations. The society validates male's sexual prowess, and female's sexual prowess is defined as "hysteria" that have been discussed by many women writers—even in the writings of Parijat and Jhamak Ghimire who are considered as disabled women writers who discuss how patriarchal society view women as inferior sex and disabled women "asexual."

In other developed countries, there are a lot of discussions and discourses on sex and gender in writing, examining how media projects sexual assault and sexual violence and its roles and weaknesses. Also, policies have been made in each institution and organization where employees need to take the course on sexual violence as soon as they are hired. They discuss the effect of sexual assault on a victim, and the language that needs to be carefully used for the victim. But we do not have such enough discussions and awareness in the context of Nepal. We do not discuss the long-term effect of such sexual assault and rape on women's body and we cannot realize what rape does to a woman's body. Talking about rape, in her article "The Careless Language of

Sexual Violence," Roxane Gay writes, "Psychologically, there are any number of effects including PTSD, anxiety, fear, coping with the social stigma, and coping with shame, and on and on. The actual rape ends but the aftermath can be very far reaching and even more devastating than the rape itself" besides physical effects such as "unwanted pregnancy and sexually transmitted diseases, vaginal and anal tearing, fistula and vaginal scar tissue…"

We need to understand culture that defines gender to assess the cases of sex and rape and how sex is different from rape, how gender roles and patriarchal cultural practices in Nepal make the topic of sex a taboo, why sex tends to be a subject of force, farce, and forgetfulness. It is the need of the hour to probe into these queries for a better assessment of sex, rape, gender, and patriarchy, especially, in the context of Nepal. (***Published in The Rising Nepal***)

How Culture Shapes Politics

———

WITHOUT CULTURE, AND the relative freedom it implies, society, even when perfect, is but a jungle. This is why any authentic creation is a gift to the future: Albert Camus.

There are many definitions about culture. In brief, cultures are our values. Cultural variations inform people differently, so is the understanding and perception of people about the world. As Camus said in the statement above, cultures are essentials to authenticate the society, but it also implies "relative freedom." If our culture cannot guarantee our freedom, such culture has no meaning. The freedom is associated with the culture of freedom of expression, of the right to live without fear, of being critical and creative and imaginative, of speaking our mind and the like.

Thus, we elect our politicians and have policies in place to guarantee the freedom, to put some bad cultures in check and balance. Although the policies are formulated to address social and cultural problems, we fail to formulate such policies to deal with such problems due to the way politicians and policymakers think and understand our culture and its significance in our lives. Following what we have witnessed, seen, observed, and learned culturally, we seldom question the bad culture, thus hindering all kinds of progress—social or cultural or political.

Upbringing

Nepal is such a place where diverse cultures are into play because its geography, ecologically speaking, is unique. However, some of the cultures are in common across the three different ecological belts, i.e. mountain, hill and the Terai. As we know, our behaviors, actions, attitudes, perceptions are based on our upbringing or the culture where we are raised. We define who we are, and our ideals based on what we eat, what we wear and other cultural values that are in practice around us. We learn those cultures looking at and observing them around us, witnessing and observing them in front of us, listening to our parents and grandparents preaching about such cultures.

Such observations are deeply rooted in our brain, and we feel the culture in our heart; we assume that going beyond such cultural practices is something unusual and bizarre and unethical. Culture guides our ideals and the way of life, demeanors, manners, and philosophy of what is good and what is bad. Whatever we consider as bad might be something very good for people from another culture. A simple example could be, especially for Hindus, because the majority of Nepali are Hindus, eating beef is considered something sinful. Thus, someone raised in Hindu culture can hardly think of consuming beef in their meal. Similarly, we join our hands to elders, instead of shaking and that already creates a hierarchy between the older and younger, so the younger one, no matter how visionary s/he is, always hesitates to share or boldly bring their perceptive with/in front of the elder ones.

We hardly encourage younger people to put forth front their perspectives. This culture is in practice in all strata of Nepali society, whether that be in the field of academia that always remains hierarchical, creating an unhealthy gap between teachers and students, or in many bureaucratic institutions, or even in politics.

Our politics and the way it is running works like a culture that teaches us morals such as loyalty, tolerance, patience, faith, and dependability. We are hardly taught to question the authority or the person in power unlike the culture in European countries where appreciation is received for being critical of the person in authority. We hardly accept the change, for example the one — who is attached to one party and the history shows his predecessor, including his grandfather and father have been voting for the same party — hesitates to vote for another party even if the leader is more visionary. It is all because the person does not want to break the tradition of remaining in the same political party and wants to continue to keep the legacy of their forefathers. The person does not want to disrespect the tradition of voting for the same political party his parents and grandparents voted for.

Our Nepali cultures place a primary emphasis on tradition and the wisdom is passed down from older generations. Such cultures show a great deal of deference and respect for parents and other elders who are the links to these past sources of knowledge or cultural practices. Such cultural practices play a pivotal role in Nepali politics too. That is the reason why we hardly find a person with strong leadership in Nepali politics. In terms of maintaining a cordial relationship, our culture mentors the rules like how to talk with whom, discouraging direct eye contact while speaking with people in authority, which is just the opposite of European cultures, discouraging a handshake with elders, and so on. A cultural belief is too much eye contact is disrespectful and even confrontational. On the other hand, in the context of American society, not making eye contact can be misconstrued as an indication of insincerity or discomfort.

Our Nepali culture is more of an I-am-the-one-so-none-can-be-critical-of-me-or-speak-bad-about-me kind of culture. This sort of tendency will boast the person in power. In our culture, there is a heightened sense of decorum and politeness to be required when meeting with the person in authority. However, our younger generation these days somewhat become critical of the government, the political party, and the leaders, trying to correct those cultures and thinking out of the box to practice the culture that guarantees people's "relative freedom."

Silent cultures

We need to keep such cultures in check and balance to understand how cultures shape politics and policies. Such silent cultures that are taken for granted are powerful to communicate strong messages. Thus, being able to acknowledge such messages may help better understand politics and policies in the making. We tend to say "a picture is worth a thousand words". Such cultures are like pictures. When analyzed its effect and impression upon our lives, we will be able to thoroughly understand the functioning of the society that guides our politics and policies. Politics without good culture is like a jungle that has a place for wild creatures. (***Published in The Rising Nepal 30 Sep, 2021***)

Let the Subaltern Speak

SOME TIME AGO, ONE of the parliamentarians questioned to my question: "Who would listen to me in the parliament?" when I asked him "Why could not you bring about any reformative change in your territory from where you were elected?" My question was regarding people's social and economic status. He was elected through the proportional voting system.

He further said, "I am bichara (poor) there. My voice is not heard. I feel like I am merely there to fill in the gaps in the parliament. I feel like I am one of the oppressed here, but I never felt so in my community."

The Subaltern

In "Can the Subaltern Speak?," Gayatri Spivak writes: "The subaltern has no history and cannot speak." According to Spivak, the subalterns are the oppressed group of people. It can be anyone among the "lowest strata of the rural gentry, impoverished landlords, rich peasants and upper middle peasants all of whom belonged, ideally speaking, to the category of "people" or "subaltern classes." All those who are oppressed cannot be subaltern, but all the subaltern can be oppressed. The subaltern can be heterogeneous in composition or demographic, and economically and socially uneven. A class, a group of people or a person "dominant in one area could be dominated in another" (Spivak).

Candidly speaking, the parliamentarian's woe was an indication that even if he was dominant and popular in his area from where he was elected through the proportional voting system, he was among the oppressed ones in the parliament, meaning nobody heard his voice. Thus, he could not truly represent his people, nor was he able to speak up, nor would anyone hear him out. This is, indeed, the situation in

Nepali politics where the majority of the politicians cannot truly represent the marginalized community, people's mandate, and their voices.

Nepali politics has historically been dominated by elitism, by certain class of people, by a "bourgeois-nationalist elitism," that merely reinforces the idea of the collective consciousness of nationalism without reaching out to the individual consciousness or the narratives of diverse Nepali citizens. It is important to understand and respect how each individual view the nation and themselves and their expectations. Nepali population is heterogeneous, demographic, and socially, culturally, economically, and linguistically diverse.

Until we hear them or the one who represents them out, certain sections of people will be left behind and will always remain oppressed, including other marginalised people, such as women, disabled, people in poverty, Dalits and so on. The certain class of people in Nepali politics fails (or chooses not) to understand that Nepal's population is diverse in terms of culture, castes, and creeds. The result will be the woes of the oppressed like how one of the parliamentarians felt.

The leaders of our nation essentialize the evenness of Nepali demography based on their perspectives and impressions without checking the facts, looking back to the past, or not going back to the source they came from or the society they lived in. Until they hear the voices and narratives coming from different people living in different strata of society, the leaders can never do good for the nation and its well-being. The master-slave narrative unconsciously hangs in the so-called leaders' mind that does not let them prioritise the voices of the subaltern in politics. The leaders think in terms of their own limited interests which Sigmund Freud might call "libidinal" instead of social or national.

The meaning of the word "libidinal" I have used here in this context is not relating to the libido or sexual, but to the economic self-interest of the politicians. In his book "Libidinal Economy (1974)," French philosopher Jean-François Lyotard uses the term referring to the systems of exchange and valuation for fantasies, desires, fears, aversions, and enjoyment.

The irony lies in Nepali politics. Political parties advocate for the rights and representations of the oppressed and the subaltern. They have brought women, disabled, homosexual, and other indigenous representatives in the parliament to represent the voices of the voiceless, to address the conditions of the people who are left on the margins, to ameliorate the conditions of the oppressed group of people. But the question is: do the oppressed have opportunity or encouragement to speak? Can they represent the marginalized, the oppressed, the subaltern? Are their voices being heard? Going back to the parliamentarian, I mentioned above: Who will speak for the marginalized? Who will hear them out? How can truly one represent the consciousness of the subaltern, their rights, and their woes?

Guided by 'self'

Some politicians in Nepal are guided by the ideology of "self" while the marginalized ones remain as others and that is exacerbating when the political representation is divided between self and other in practice. This will continue to pressurize the marginalized/oppressed to follow the ones in power and watch the politics of the oppressor.

Yes, after many political movements and upheavals, we have noticed that political parties raise the issue of the "subaltern," but that doesn't seem to be materialized yet besides being able to fulfil their own personal interests. However, they continue to keep their agendas up for their popularity, and that will continue to create an illusion of what they are going to do is to create a "good society." When they don't do what they say, it is high time we knew their intentions and penalise them in the election using our voting rights.

Let's think about politics: Can the subaltern speak? (***Published in the rising Nepal 22 Nov, 2021***)

Nepali Literature and its Promising Future

LAST YEAR, WHEN I RETURNED to America, Peshal Pokhrel, my friend and also a Nepali immigrant in the US asked me for a favor if I could bring him some newly published Nepali books including Durga Subedi's Biman Bidroha (An Airplane revolt), Jagat Nepal's B P Ko Bidroha (BP's revolt), Sushila Karki's Nyaya (Justice) and others. He was very happy to have them from me.

It is heartening to learn that Nepali literature is travelling across the world, not only because of the growing readership or because of the emerging translation of major historical, representative, and most current fictional and non-fictional works by leading Nepali writers, such as Guru Prasad Mainali, Laxmi Prasad Devekota, Parijat, Jhamak Ghimire and others, but also because of a wider readership across the globe for two reasons: one, the works that have been translated into English have access to many people who read and write in English; two, increasing Nepali emigrants across the world have a tendency to buy and read Nepali/English books and share their contents with their fellows or lend them the books to read. If there was no access to these translated books and no tendency to read, there wouldn't be this much of travel of Nepali literature across the globe. Profuse online media have made Nepali literature travel as the number of online readership is growing vehemently.

We also have seen a number of publication houses, that has started publishing good fictional and non-fictional books and that have a practice of gatekeeping before the acceptance of the submitted manuscript, growing in recent years, for example Fine Print and BookHill and others. To make the books and different publications available across the globe, technology and other online platforms have made this much easier. If we need to read a Nepali book or the book translated into English while in abroad, one can easily order certain books from amazon, an American multinational technology company based in Seattle that focuses on e-commerce, cloud computing, digital streaming, and artificial intelligence. One can also directly publish a book via Kindle Publishing and make it available via amazon.

I have seen many Nepali books or the books translated into English made available on amazon where anyone can have access to if they want to receive either a hardcopy or a digital one. I have seen on amazon Krishna Dharabasi's Radha, a translated version of Nepali Radha novel, Sanjeev Upreti's recently published Nepali version of Hansa, or Gopal Parajuli's "Proposal for a New World: An Epic Poem," an English translation of Nepali epic poem, and, not to mention, many others. Not only does this show the availability of books via many platforms and growing readership of Nepali literary and non-literary works across the world, but also it reflects on the promising future of the growing readership and the travels of Nepali literature and culture.

One of the interesting things that have been happening in Nepali literature, as I mentioned, currently is translation. Translation is not an easy job because it requires a correct cultural interpretation and right translation of the writing originated in the culture where the author was born and raised to the language which the author might have never thought of, played with or acted upon. Culture is seeped through the language, and it is not easy to translate that culture into the language which, at times, may never exist in the original language the text was written.

Translation demands patience, perseverance, research, sensitivity, and the practice of walking into the shoes of others' culture. However, Mahesh Paudyal, a young writer, critic, and translator has been doing an amazing job in the context of translation. He has been profusely translating many works, such as Krishna Dharabasi's Radha, other major representative Nepali stories, and many others. There are others, such as Ramchandra K.C. who has translated many English stories into Nepali and Nepali into English, such as Kaflka's Metamorphosis in Nepali and "Rebel," a collection Nepali war stories translated into English and made them available on Amazon.

I myself have translated Shakespeare's short stories edited by Charles and Mary Lamb into Nepali as "Shakespear ka kathaharu." The question now is: is this enough for Nepali literature to travel across the world and attain a wider readership? How much can we be positive in the context of growing readership across the world? Can we be content with what has been happening in terms of growing readership and translation of Nepali to English and vice versa?

"Actually, we should not only focus on translating Nepali into English or English into Nepali with an idea that it would help our literature and culture travel, but also we should practice translating other languages into Nepali for our literature to grow more, and that is what I learned from some conferences and seminars with many publishers at international book fairs," Keshav Parajuli, Managing Director of Bhuni Puran Puplication House told me in a meeting with him the other day. It reminded me of a book "Khubuj," a beautiful novel of a heart wrenching story of a person who goes to an Arabian country for a job and ends up being abused, but he survives a tumultuous, scary, and pathetic journey of life, translated from English into Nepali by Dinesh Kafle who is also translating Nayan raj Pandey's "Ular" into English. Originally, the book "Khubuj" was written into the Malayalm language with a title "Goat days" in English so although Kafle did a great job by translating the book into Nepali, it was not actually translated into Nepali from Malayalam directly so there might have been many things lost in translation.

The Nepali publication houses may cultivate such talents and translators who can directly translate not only from English to Nepali or vice versa, but from many other languages into Nepali too. In this regard, Keshav Parajuli resonates one more time. He asked me if I could find any publication house in America or a foreign land that would be willing to pay me for translating their works into Nepali language. Although I had no idea about that but Parajuli also shared another knowledge with me that some Chinese or Turkish publishers would be willing to pay for translating their works into Nepali and even pay royalty to the translator.

I wonder if Nepali book publishers can do that for those who would be willing to translate not only into English from Nepali or from Nepali to English but from Nepali to many other languages. Perhaps, this practice might make Nepali literature travel beyond what we could imagine, and we could be even more hopeful about its promising future. How/what could International Nepali Literature Society think about it beyond merely holding conferences every year in different countries and publishing a few books here and there that are hardly recognized in an international arena? (***Published in The Rising Nepal, Feb 21, 2020***)

Research Matters to Development

THE WORD "RESEARCH" is derived from the Middle French "recherche," which means "to go about seeking" and the earliest recorded use of the term was in 1577. Its role is attached to the development of nation states. Research is important not only for the lives of people hailing from all racial, cultural, and socio-economic backgrounds, but also for the economic and social development of countries across the globe. It contributes to the development of nationhood in the field of science and technology, arts and humanities, and many other implicit and explicit areas that we might have hardly imagined. We have seen how developed countries progressed because they make high investments in research.

A few days ago, Policy Research Institute (PRI), a Nepal government think tank, that was established in 2018 with the purpose of studying and analyzing existing policies and possible future policies in various fields, invited different research institutions working in the field of research and development to share with, suggest to, and support PRI in their specialized ways. A further goal of PRI is to recommend and suggest policies to the government and make her responsible, accountable, and transparent in the process of forming policies to implementing them at many levels of the bureaucracy, which is inextricably tied to economic, social, and cultural development of the country.

Around 20 of the participants, each representing their institutions, attended the program. I also, representing Nexus Institute for Research and Innovation (NIRI), joined the conversation around the table in the presence of national and international researchers including Pro. Dr. Bishnu Raj Upreti, an acting chairperson of PRI and Surendra Labh, a former PRI board member and current National Planning Commission member who even oversees research.

Idea of research

All the conversation and the topic of discussion revolved around the idea of research and development and how research is one and only route to reach where we find the development of nation. "However, these days research seems to be a synonym of development, and, therefore, the research does not appear to be as effective as it supposed to be," Uttam Babu Shrestha, the founding director of the Global Institute for Interdisciplinary Studies (GIIS) argued: "I, at times, feel like a research consultant." Shrestha has been doing much research in the field. He also emphasized the idea that there is no development without quality research.

Many of the participants brought up the topic of funding and the risk of being influenced by foreign donors who might have vested interests in research if one is not careful, and such research with vested interests could do harm for the development of the nation. PRI also opined to discourage such funding for the betterment of society and the country. Many of them suggested that PRI should follow certain guidelines and make the policies inclusive in terms of participating researchers, making the research environment encouraging, preparing for a long-term strategic plan for research (for example what the research would be like after ten years from now), recognising traditional, local, and community knowledge, forming policies and identifying their importance, running trainings and workshops, and thinking about the sector of public health.

Finally, the discussion emphasized two things: the "mapping of research" and the "quality of research" to ensure the development of the nation. Dr. Upreti highlighted PRI's role as a guiding body in policy research and emphasized the integration of three kinds of knowledge in research — indigenous, bureaucratic, and intellectual — while in policy making.

Some of participants even brought up the idea of public-private partnership in research and its effectiveness, while others talked about establishing an encouraging environment for researchers who are willing to come back to Nepal, the effective atmosphere could be established by forming a policy that allows bringing in equipment for labs from abroad tax free and fund researchers for at least three to five years along with salaries and benefits.

Although many in the discussion talked about funding and all kinds of research, none spoke about the difficulty in finding funders for social science research, especially in the field of arts and humanities and literature and creative writing that basically aim to explore the soft side of humanity. I broached the topic and tried to explain the significance of literature to understand society, politics, and even economics and the existing reality is the scarcity of funding compared to the hard sciences.

Policy mismatch

Reflecting on the works of literature, we could better understand society, people, and economics from people who lived their lives and policymakers could formulate such policies that could address the conditions of those people. I even gave them an example of my Ph.D. research that analyzed the creative works by women with disabilities in Nepal, such as Jhamak Ghimire and Bishnu Kumari Waiwa and reflected on the existing policies, and I finally found a policy gap along with some policy mismatches. Should there be enough funding for such research, we could explore the tacit knowledge and implicit aspects of people and society.

The policies that have been formulated should be brought into practice, then we must observe its impact and review —most of the participants in the discussion emphasized this key necessity. Overall, research matters to any nation wishing to make strides toward greater development. All the research institutions in the nation should cooperate and be geared towards research and development. Thus, research matters. (***Published in The Rising Nepal Dec 22, 2021***)

Dealing with the Death

RECENTLY, QUEEN ELIZABETH II died at the age of 96 after the longest reign in the history of monarchs on the British throne. "Long live the King." Two years ago, my wife lost her parents who died young. When your immediate family members die, it is very hard for you to turn the tragedy into a creative force and into your own strength. After all, what is death? Why is it hard to accept? How can one deal with it?

Knowing about Death

Many philosophers have viewed death as a good friend of human beings and invite us to discuss death sincerely. It is something that needs to be celebrated. In this context, a famous 20th century American singer, lyricist, and musician Jimi Henderson, in his song, writes—

I'm the one that has to die

when it's time for me to die,

so let me live my life,

the way I want to.

Rich, poor, lucky or unlucky ones—all of them must leave this world one day. All the emperors, you name them, surrender in front of death. A Danish writer Christian Anderson writes that only to live in life is not enough until one lives with joy and bloom. Similarly, a famous American doctor Martin H Fisher defines life as a ticket that allows one to watch a cinema of/on the earth. These ideas help us understand that life and death are interdependent. Where there is life there is death. There is the immediate and intimate relationship between life and death. There is no guarantee of the who, what, when, where, how of a person's death.

Why does a human being fear death when one knows it is sure to come? One is always running away from death, always scared of it, but death doesn't leave the person. In his article "Mrityu chintan, death contemplation," Tekendra Adhikari writes that although the person knows about the surety of death, there are a few reasons why the person wants to run away from it. The reasons are due to 1. the psychology of fear 2. the lack of good relationship between human and nature, and 3. the greed, selfish love, anger, and jealousy.

That is the same death, which took the Queen away or my wife's parents away, will come to take us away one day. The only thing is we don't know when the death comes for sure in terms of the exact date—time, day, month, and year. After we know that, the statement of Martin H Fisher's remains significant. He says, "Why should we be afraid of death? Isn't it a beautiful experience one could ever have in life? Isn't the death the final truth?" We may not be sure whether a child will be born or not, but when the child is born it is sure that the child will die.

Some of us are frequently questioning "What, after all, do we mean by living a meaningful life?" "What makes human life meaningful?" We hardly get answers to such questions. Great writers, poets, philosophers, thinkers have spent many years to discern the meaning of life and live it. American-born British poet T. S. Elliot in his poem "The Waste Land" looks for humanity while revealing the meaninglessness and loneliness of life. Elliot hints on the idea that in this physical world, people have been selfish and forlorn, and the ultimate solution of it is to establish the relationship of humanity and fraternity that prevent the person from being lonely. A Russian writer Vladmir Nabokov reveals our consciousness about how pain and tragedy make us stern and unkind. Joseph Conrad's opinion is how human lives are affected if there does persist miss-communication about life. Reading what these thinkers and writers have said, we understand that to live a meaningful life is to establish human relationships, to understand the pain of others and other miscellaneous things that have directly or indirectly affected human lives, such as the death, in this context.

Importance of Moral Capacity

In the New York Times best seller book "When Breaths Become Air," Paul Kalanithi, who was a neurosurgeon by profession and became a writer later— who died before he turned 40 due to cancer— writes that he read literature and philosophy to understand what makes life meaningful; he read neuroscience to understand how the brain gives a human being the strength to understand the meaning of the world. He worked in the lab and established a good relationship with his friends. There are some people who do many things to understand life and make it meaningful—some do magic, some discover things, some do social works, some establish a good relationship with people. Have we ever taken enough time to think about bringing in a good relationship with people around and on behalf of humanity? Have we ever discussed the topics of pain in human lives and how to address it? Such questions will help us understand life and death and their relationships. Kalanithi writes, "The questions of life and death are the human moral questions." Death is not an easy topic to deal with and to discuss. Kalanithi who himself was a neurosurgeon saw many deaths in front of him and convinced and consulted many of his patients, but later he himself found it hard to deal with his own death, and, finally, he revealed saying, "I helped my patients understand about pain, but when I was in pain and suffered from cancer, the understanding of the pain was way more than how I understood it before. Those were the two different experiences—to be a doctor and treat the patient and to be myself a patient and go see the doctor. The doctor never would realize the pain of the patient." Thomas Browne in his book "Religio

Medici" writes "The way we come to this world with pain and force, then we would know thing, but after we come to this world, it is very hard to come out of it."

To be born and to die is indispensable for nature must run its course. An absurdist dramatists Samuel Backet writes "One day we are born and one day we will die." To live a meaningful life, only the knowledge on the topic wouldn't be enough, we need a moral clarity and the capacity to understand death. There is a word in Greek language "arete" which means capacity that demands emotional, mental, and physical capacity. The person who is in impending death has the greatest fear of his identity and existence—"now I will never come back to this earth," "I won't be able to see anyone," "I will lose all my people" and so on. But if the person has a good relationship with his people during his lifetime and he becomes sure of his importance and identity in society even after his death tomorrow, such understanding might ease the person's death. The human relationship is important during the time of tragedy, but the person fails to understand that because we are becoming more selfish and materialistic. The person thinks more about the material things, less about the moral deeds and inspirational works that could make a human life meaningful before they would die. If you find someone who could be by your side, hold your hand, that perhaps will make you go with a smile although one knows it is very hard to take death comfortably. Even a morally capable person finds it very difficult. Martin Heidegger says, "to know that the time is passing is the state of boredom," but on the contrary to realize the inevitability of death all the time is the search for meaningfulness in life. All the living beings face death sooner or later, but to look for meaning within it is to look for one's identity and existence within it.

Although we are perfect within ourselves, this world is not complete and perfect, and we must be able to accept that. Yes, we forget everything when we are in pain. We forget to be who we are. We do not become subjects but turn into objects when we are in pain. We are obliged to be under the control of pain, but to feel, to realize ourselves within the pain is to live a meaningful life. Nietzsche says, "the real life is the life of pain." George Bataille writes that "death is the symbol of life, way to infinity." Nepali maestro Narayan Gopal sings a song:

Kehi mitho bata gara raat taysai dhalkadaichh/Bhaere feri ekantama runuta chhadaichh (Please talk something nice as the evening is turning into night/Anyway we are going to cry in solitude after all.

Conclusion: Meaningful Death

When you can define your life and make it meaningful even at the mouth of death, that is the meaningful life you are living. Even if the writer Kalanithi knew that he was dying, he wrote "I must learn to live differently. Death is an inevitable wanderer so to know that I am dying until I die is the real living." To make our live a meaningful is a moral responsibility. Sometimes we fail to accept death even if we understand and realize it, but even if those who do not accept death before and accepts it at the end, that still makes the person's life meaningful. Science can save us to some extent, but until we have the moral capacity, neither we can have any hope for anything, nor can we face fear of death, nor can we remain happy. Thus, we must receive the knowledge of how we behave with people and establish relationships with them. We fear death and that is natural, but because of the fear we hardly discuss death. To discuss it is to understand it, the meaning of it, to find the identity and existence of what it means to live, to openly accept it, take the death as life. An international Book prize winner Gitanjali Shree in her novel "Tomb of sand" writes addressing the condition of a 80-year-old woman, a character in the novel who is in depression after she lost her husband, but she regains hope and strength later—One can mourn, but what is gone is gone.

The death of my parents-in-law not only helped me understand death and its effect on their daughters, but also taught me to love them even more, respect them, and know the meaning of "take care" in one's life. Such lessons are meaningful in life. If we learn such things in life, we can also give some meanings to death and can frankly tell why death comes and why it is meaningful—it unites and reunites the relatives and friends, makes us be around the dead body and contemplate life and death, increases humanity, and establishes emotional relationships among relatives and helps us think of them through memories. I recall these lines from Edwin Leibfreed.

For death is but a passing phase of Life;

A change of dress, a disrobing;

A birth into the unborn again;

A commencing where we ended;

A starting where we stopped to rest;

A crossroad of Eternity;

A giving up of something, to possess all things.

The end of the unreal, the beginning of the real... (Oct 10, 2022)

Section: Two

(A collection of short articles that reflect on human soft sides and nostalgia)

Drawing a parallel between Bhupi and Whitman

———

HUNDAIN BIHAN MIRMIRE tara jharer nagaye, bandaina muluk dui chara saput marer nagaye (Morning will never come if at dawn a few stars don't fall down, a nation will not progress if a few of its sons don't sacrifice their lives.)

This line is Nepali poet Bhupi Serchan's dedication to nation and nationality like the 19th century American poet Walt Whitman celebrating individualism and democratic idealism in his ballads:

I celebrate myself, and sing myself, And what I assume you shall assume, For every atom belonging to me as good belongs to you.

The ego "I" is substituted for collective feelings. The poem comprises the self and society, people and landscape. That is what we see in Bhupi Sechan's patriotic poems too.

Tara you desh timro jatikai mero pani desh ho (Just as his country is yours, so is it mine).

Both poets share their common theme: both expound on the theme of humanity and democracy. They believe that humanity never dies. It is reincarnated in different forms as Bhupi Sherchan says:

Tara manabata mardaina tyo feri palaaunchh (Humanity dies not die, but grows again in your heart.)

And Whitman finds humanity reflected in the leaves of grass:

Or I guess the grass is itself a child, the produced babe of the vegetation.

Or I guess it is a uniform hieroglyphic,

And it means, Sprouting alike in broad zones and narrow zones,

Growing among black folks as among white...

Both feel it is easier to die than to live. Sherchan writes:

Marer jane haru ho jier ta hera, Jiuna jhan kati garo chh (Those who have died, try living once it is harder to live)

Bhupi Sherchan's 'Main battiko Shikha" (The light of a candle), "Gumne Mech maathi andho manche" (A blind man in a swirling chair) and Walk Whitman's "Leaves of Grass" are creations that show a certain path for the future of nation and nationality. Although Bhupi Sherchan is a 20th century poet, his ideas on nation and nationality are parallel to those that Whitman held. Sherchan's identification of trinity in one maps the cyclical process of life—ma ek putra, ek pati ra ek pita hun (I am a son, a husband, and a father).

Whitman talks of similar things in a different way. Their poems are the aware of the social political situation. They express agony, anguish, and the irony remains as fresh as ever with concrete visual symbols that narrate their own experiences of life. They said that good and evil are the inherent parts of human life. Wisdom does not lie in rejection of veil, but in acceptance of both.

Although, as poets, they have much in common, in the end, two individuals remain separate. Whitman transcendence the individual through knowledge of integration, wholeness, and continuity of life, death and beauty of the living world. His poems end optimistically.

I stop somewhere waiting for you (From "Songs of Myself"). Sherchan doesn't see the integration of life and ends at pessimistic tone.

Aatmahatya garna baadhya hunechhu (It will be necessary for me to take my own life, from "Letter to Ho Chi Minh). (***Published in the Himalayan Times)***

Magic of Music

"YEKLAI BASDA SANDHAI Malai,Samjhana Timro Aaidinchha,

Sahana Nasaki Aankha Bata Aansu Tesai Jhari Dinchha"

(I remember you all the time when I am alone, I cannot bear it and tears roll down by themselves.)

This song is sung by Aruna Lama, composed by Dev Bajracharya and the music rendered by Ganesh and Ratna. It is one of the most heart touching songs.I do not know in which context the song was composed but I always associate the song with my brother, Cheban, who always used to be with me during our childhood. Today, we have both grown up. We do not have time to play games such as making sandcastles or making dolls of bride and bridegroom. He is busy from morning to evening and so am I. We both have become mechanized now. We no longer have the childish freedom that we had. Although I still like to play such games, some social norms and values restrict us. If we play such games now, we will be objects of ridicule. And I just silently weep like a child missing those childhood days.

It is music that fulfills my desire for childhood. There are many other songs that touch me; either Narayan Gopal's Jhareko Pata Jastai Bhayo Uzad Mero Jindagi or Bhakta Raj Acharya's Yo Katha Suru Garera Khana... and the like. There are many more evergreen songs, which make me more enthusiastic.Music is really pleasing to the ears of any being. I have read that cattle used to stop grazing when Lord Krishna used to play his flute. Doubtless, this is the magic of music. Music cures mental or psychiatric diseases. It can also fulfill the thirst of love of unrequited lovers. I wonder what power music has! It can reunite departed lovers And betrayed lovers best consolation is to listen to music. Music enables one to look at life positively.

Music acts as your friend when you are alone. Everyone likes music either in happiness or in sorrow. I remember the poetic lines from Walles Steven's "Peter Quince At the Clavier."

"Just as my finger on the keys,

Make music, so the selfsame sounds,

On my spirit make a music, too."

It is music that fills the human heart with zeal and enthusiasm. It not only entertains the people but also encourages them and adds more power to the spirit. It adds freshness and energy to life. Life becomes something else. Who can say that it does not have supernatural power?

Music refreshes a tired heart. When the sense of pessimism and failure arise, it is music that provides optimism and makes life complete. (*Published Thursday November, 11 2004 Source: The Kathmandu Post*)

Love Animals

"LIBERTY IS GIVEN BY nature even to mute animals"— Tacitus

One day, a big black cat, all of a sudden, crossed the street while my friend and I were on our way to Gausala on foot.

Without any delay, my friend picked up a stone and hurled at it and pronounced the very word "bad luck". He not only postponed the plan of heading to Gausala for the special purpose but also made the cat severely maimed. The cat merely mewed and what I was watching was bleeding from head.

The cat was almost gored to death. The cat disappeared but I didn't know whether the cat died or survived. This is a minor incident that I witnessed but there are dozens of such incidents that have been taking place, directly or indirectly where the lives of many creatures are at risk.

The plight is more pathetic and painful. This is all because of encroaching humans, which has brought the lives of animals on the verge of extinction.

Nevertheless, the incident reminds me that many pet animals have been tortured and killed for no proper reason. Many of them have become the victims of superstitious belief. Just take for instance, more than 40,000 bulls are killed every year in the bull-fight in the world. Many animals are used as guinea pig. Around ten million animals are butchered worldwide per year for human consumption and appeasement.

Thousands of buffaloes, goats and chickens are brought into Kathmandu from different parts of the country in such a ruthless way that many of them get severely wounded before they reach Kathmandu and some of them lose their lives on the way.

Every year, thousands of animals are given up to appease Gods and goddesses in the name of Panchabali - sacrifice of five different creatures such as pigs, buffaloes, goats, roosters and rats.

God has made man powerful of all creatures. But that does not mean that we can behave with animals the way we like. Animals also feel soreness when beaten just like us. The only difference is that we can express, complain, communicate, and they cannot.

Cruelty towards the animals is a boastful manner. If we love them, we understand their emotion, needs and affinity. We have to stop the violence against animals.

Animals too understand the language of love and empathy. Animals being loyal and affable play a vital role for human existence as well. And how human treats them determines the existence of the whole universe.

Let me raise the query: "Who is going to speak for those mute animals who can't speak for themselves? Love animals. They are our forefathers. (*Published Friday March, 18 2005 Source: The Kathmandu Post*)

Of Teachers and Tetchy Tykes

SOME STUDENTS BACKBITE that you are not a good teacher," one of my colleagues confided. For one who seeks approval of each student, such callous comments were both embarrassing and heart-rending. For a long time afterwards, I felt disappointed and dejected.

When I thought about it afterwards, I was able to come up with two kinds of students. Thought this might seem a naive exercise, I differentiated them into the "good" and the "bad" lots. The bad eggs were irregular in class and aggressive towards their teachers. The ones who never bothered with their homework and raised a din in the class. And these fellows wanted a lot of "liberty."

You might say that I might always scold and punish them for their bad behaviour. Umm. If so, you have never taught modern students. There is an unsaid pact among the backbenchers that a scold (or worse, some kind of physical violence) on the part of the teachers will be soundly reciprocated by boxes and punches outside the confines of the school. Hence a teacher disciplines his pupils only at the risk of his own life.

On the other hand, there are a handful of students who are gentle, disciplined, and attentive in class. These fellows understand their responsibilities as students very well. They also routinely do their assignments and homework. Unsurprisingly, they have good relationships with the teachers. These are the students that every teacher labors for.

It can be a hard balance between fulfilling all responsibilities of a good teacher while at the same time knowing that no matter how hard you try, there will be some students who will never improve. I feel bad at not being able to make them see the importance of education and respect for the elders. But there is little I can do. If someone closes both his ears and simply refuses to listen to anyone else, whose fault is it that they never hear what they should?

A good teacher, I believe, also has to be a good student. He has as much to learn from the students as he has to impart to them. But in modern-day classrooms, increasingly filled with deaf and dumb students, the teacher can do little beside sit aside and wonder about the sorry future of their sorry students. (***Published Wednesday March, 21 2007, Source: The Himalayan Times***)

Bitter Truth

AS OLDER OF THE TWO children in the family, I have huge responsibilities on my shoulders. I shudder at the very thought of not being able to live up to my parents' expectations. Besides my family, I also have other things to think about: when to get married, when to have kids, how to save money for that day when I will have even more people to look after... a thousand thoughts jostle for space and confuse my mind.

But my parents are helpless too. Who else can they depend on to take care of them in their old age? And who else, except their eldest child, is there to share their feelings with?

Sometimes, when the pressure really gets to me, I lock myself up and cry silently. At other times, I think about going abroad, leaving everyone. The more I think about my responsibilities, the more desperate I get and try to come up with crazy escapist ideas. At these times, I feel pain grip my very heart and benumb my brain. Then the question pops up in my mind: Am I being too ambitious? Am I then an escapist to dream about going abroad for my doctorate; being rich and purchasing a luxurious apartment in Kathmandu; getting married to a beautiful and intelligent girl; being a mini-celebrity... a guitarist in a big-bad rock band, for example.

Then, I recall Willy Loman, that miserable character in Arthur Miller's play Death of a Salesman who could never make his dreams come true. He never got rich, his name was never printed in the papers, he was not regarded as the "finest man" that ever lived. None of his big expectations were fulfilled till the end of his life. One day he leaves the world, his umpteen dreams unfulfilled.

This might sound like a cop out, but I have come to realize that the greatest lesson one can learn in life is to compromise. In fact, it constitutes the very essence of living. If not, what alternative is there to surrendering to your negative mental vibes? Giving up on things you have lived your whole life for is by no means easy. It won't be a cakewalk for me either. But at the same time, I have also come to realize that if I try, there is no reason I should not be able to come good on my parents' expectations only if I could somehow mesh my desires with theirs. (***Published in The Himalayan Times Published: June 11, 2007***)

Brother and Sister

I LOVE HER VERY MUCH. It is with her that I have shared countless plates of meal, fruits, and vegetables. What I like about her the most is that, unlike yours truly, she manages to keep up her smile even while under stress and hardship. If she is unable to cope with any of her problems, she seeks my help.

Besides finding my presence soothing, she says she greatly values my suggestions. No matter how angry I am, her smile melts my wrath away in a trice. But how does she manage to keep her cool even while I ridicule and tease her with names like Kali, Pudki, and Bhunti? Need I say then that I too find her presence comforting? Indeed, my sister has a thing or two to teach to her naive brother. No matter what one of us is doing, the other never feels disturbed. With so much influence over me, she is my source of inspiration. Any surprise? Now we can guess what the other is thinking just by looking at each other's face.

I love her because she is sensitive but honest, childlike but illuminating. Even while I guide her, I am always learning something in turn. Hence, when, one day, out of the blue, she blurted out that she didn't like me, I was completely dumbfounded and heartbroken. How could someone I admired and loved so much say something so callous, so hurtful? I couldn't understand. That day, I could not sleep for the whole night. I tried to find solace in other things, but nothing would cheer me up.

But early next day, she came up to me, bubbling and smiling as always and planted a kiss on my cheek. "Dada! I love you very much". It was then that I realized what a unique relationship we shared. It was a heartbreak the day before and patch up the next. We couldn't keep from talking to each other for more than a day or two. I guess no other relationship is as precious and pure as that between a brother and a sister.

In times of hardships, there is nothing like having someone as sympathetic as a sister to narrate my woes to. I hope the ever-changing times will have no impact upon our relationship. If, for any reason, misunderstanding created a chasm between the two of us, I am sure, I would remain a miserable person no matter what other worldly things might come my way. (***Published in The Himalayan Times Nov 28, 2006***)

Culture Vulture

SOMETIMES BACK A PHOTOGRAPH published in a national daily attracted my attention. The photograph depicted a festival celebrated by the residents of Khokana located in the south of the Kathmandu valley where they were ripping apart a live goat.

As a matter of fact, what they were doing was a part of their culture. The very next day after Gaijatra a goat is flung into Deu-pond (Pond of Gods) near the local Rudrayani temple. Some strong and fit men are chosen by the community to enter the pond to locate the animal. Holding on to whatever part they can grasp, ear, tail, hoof or head, the men start to tear the goat apart. Gripped with the fever of ripping apart the animal, even biting it, the men are oblivious to its cries of shock and pain.

Just imagine the sight of a goat being torn apart with hands and teeth. For the members of this community, it is a part of their culture and tradition. But to others, the scene would appear to be barbaric and grotesque. We also have other traditions like the Deuki system in which one of the daughters of a family is made to serve God in a temple. Then there is another festival in which some men pierce their tongues with iron needles. It is about time we gave a serious thought to such traditions.

According to a western school of thought the civilization is based on culture. People define themselves in terms of ancestry, religion, language, history, values, customs, and institutions. They identify themselves with cultural groups, tribes, ethnic groups, religious communities, nations, and, at the broadest level, civilization. Can those following this type of culture be a part of civilization? We call ourselves civilized and consider ourselves to be superior as compared to other living beings. By accepting such traditions, the unpalatable truth remains that the so-called civilized and superior being called man has been encouraging the ignorant section towards barbaric behavior.

Do such practices gel with modern thinking? The notion that man is a superior living creature appears to be a fallacy. After all, to murder an innocent creature is a heinous act. Cannot we follow a culture which is positive towards life? (**Published in** *The Himalayan Times* **Sep 12, 2005**)

Duty and Beauty

SILA AND TARA LIVE with me in Kathmandu. The former is my uncle's daughter while the latter is my own sister. I love them equally, but they refuse to follow my instructions. I wish my sisters to be successful in life, but they want me to leave them alone.

To them traditional dresses and lifestyle are obsolete, and they want to try modern dresses and enjoy the goodies. But I suggest them to follow Mahatma Gandhi's philosophy of simple living and high thinking. I try to teach them moral values, but they forget the lessons the very next day. My sisters want to ape sophisticated girls. They too want to wear short hair, dye their hair, use heavy perfume and powder, thread their eyebrows, apply heavy lipstick, and wear tight T-shirts, trousers, and pencil-heel shoes.

They never think rationally that the applying of cosmetics can do nothing to enhance their inner beauty but can cause skin allergy like itching, rashes etc. It is merely a waste of time and money. My sisters could instead utilize their money in buying books as Thoreau had once said: "Wear an old coat and buy new books."

My sisters could visit any of the religiously, culturally, and historically important places and gain knowledge in the process. However, their behaviour is exactly the opposite. They love talking to their contemporaries and forget their duty. They don't realize that duty and beauty cannot go together. For them I am not an ideal brother. They consider the enjoyments of life to be shorter, so they want to cherish the present moment. But I think that it is important to leave one's footprints for future generations to follow.

Perhaps, my sisters are right in their own way. It is difficult for two people of opposite ideas to live together. Still, I am their brother, and it is my duty to show them the right path. A brother should behave like a father, mother, and a friend as well.

Hope one day my dream of making my sisters the followers of well-regarded personalities like Mother Teresa, or a courageous lady like Pasang Lhamu Sherpa, and helpers of Florence Nightingale will come to fruition. Changing others' thoughts and beliefs are not an easy task. (**Published in *The Himalayan Times* Feb 7, 2006**)

The English Teacher

ONE OF MY BETTER FRIENDS, Thakur, who is an English teacher, was sharing his bittersweet experiences with me the other day. He complained of his meagre salary despite working for nearly ten hours a day, teaching in different schools and colleges.

"I lead a miserable life," he complained. "The perks are nearly not enough to make ends meet." The money spent on food, rent and other essentials consumes the bulk of his meagre salary. "I have not given up the big dreams I left my village with," he recalled. He had come to Kathmandu in search of better opportunities. His plight reminds me of life's endless frustrations that come with increasing responsibilities as one grows up.

My friend sometimes abhors his profession. But he has found some satisfaction in his calling. "The students give me great respect. There is nothing more precious than this. That, in turn, builds a strong bond between us." Nevertheless, most of the times, he wants to leave everything and hunt for greener pastures abroad. My friend keeps changing his mind. He wants to do so many things but cannot make up his mind while burdened with all the responsibilities that he has to shoulder.

He never tires of blaming the government for not being able to respond to the people's aspirations expressed through the recent Jana Andolan II. He holds corruption, groupism, and sycophancy responsible for most of the ills the nation is suffering from. With his constant tirades against nearly everything under the sun, Thakur reminds me of a character, Krishna, in RK Narayan's novel, The English Teacher, in many ways. The desolate character frets endlessly over his life. At thirty, he resolves to cease to live like a cow, but is continually bereft of the feeling of a great chasm in his life.

Most of Thakur's friends face a similar plight, continually dissatisfied and complaining about what they do and the meagre sum they pocket at the end of the month. But they have every reason to hold their heads high. What greater satisfaction can there be than to see the students grow under their care? Being an English teacher myself, I know what my friend is talking about. (**Published in** *The Himalayan Times* **Aug 14, 2006**)

Refreshing the Mood

BEING SEATED ON A REVOLVING chair inside the office of my friend's Newton Institute, I moved my head from right to left and as slowly as the watch's minute hand and exactly in the manner a movie cameraman moves his camera from pan right to pan left. The first object that I saw was the hanging mirror reflecting my dejected and forlorn visage mocking at my hypocrisy and just above it was a round wall clock showing a 180 degree line made by the minute and hour hands.

Next was a portrait of Gautam Buddha in his meditating posture that seemed to remind all of the importance of peace and tranquility. Very interestingly, the painting framed in rectangular size and pasted against the wall was of Sir Isaac Newton, a great British scientist who introduced the theory of gravity.

My sight slowly fell upon a date sticker glued on a wooden box reading "Thursday" evermore and made me chuckle (no one would replace the very date that would be humorous). Off mood, I turned to the side where a painting named "Prince Siddhartha bids a farewell" was positioned in the corner hanging vertically. As long as my head swept, I found a rack full of books related to GRE and TOEFEL located against the wall, and just below was a hanging picture of Saraswati, the Goddess of knowledge, holding a beena and a book.

Gradually the opened window pulled me to the world outside where a couple of lovers, I suppose, were going around the Baudha gumba, reminding me of the barren life without any girl-friend during the 24 springs of my life. I, therefore, did not pay any heed to the absence of any one damsel's love that my heart knowing or unknowingly craved for.

No sooner had my eyes caught the attention of the postcard pasted on the wall that read "when love and skill work together expect miracles" than it produced the flood of nostalgia and powerful emotion bottled up inside the core of my heart. I remembered a girl who had gently kissed my forehead as a gust of her love, had eloped with someone else, causing a landslide making the moment unforgettable for me. The door was opened, and above it was again written "Each day be happy and free". I concluded, Yeah! Cheer up. (**Published in *The Himalayan Times* March 28, 2006**).

Sarangi

THE PERFECTLY HARMONIZED words with the music produced from the strings of Sarangi, a Gaine (person who sings by playing the Sarangi) sings: *Jaati pitchhau pita baru tehi malai sahi chha, bhabanama chota lage antarghata hundu rai chha, maryo malai nisthuri mayale* (you can slap me if you want. Being injured emotionally means to suffer heartache. Malicious love marred me). He sings in his melodious and mellifluous voice. The song is so powerful that I am almost nostalgic. Like D H Lawrence wrote in his poem "Piano" thus: "my manhood is cast down in the flood of remembrance. I weep like a child for the past." I just cannot help being emotional by the melodious Sarangi tune. I hear this Gaine singing incessantly and fall in love with him and his music.

He holds me spellbound. I stop and stand as a statue, and then stare at his musical instrument. Surely, he is a Gaine who is sharing his sorrows and miseries, dreams and desires with the pedestrians. He lives on the footpath, selling his throat and art, and scrounging for whatever little he can amass. All this he does not for entertainment, but to earn his daily bread and butter. Unfortunately, no passer-by even looks at him. I count only ten rupees collected on his handkerchief spread on the floor. I add five rupees to it, but I he needs not less than Rs 30 for dinner at night, I guess.

I cannot let go of his sight. His spontaneous song spills over on the themes of betrayed lovers, tragedy of common man and the story of Ramayana, Mahabharata and Muna Madan. I listen to each of them in awe and curiosity and cannot control the tears rolling down my cheeks. His song reflects time, place, and circumstances. However, no one pays attention as if they can hardly understand the music, which bridges the generational gap. I guess the Bandbaza and remix songs have supplanted the folk music of its identity. Sarangi interprets the ups and downs as well as ebb and flow of human life. It unfolds the story of many common folks who live miserable lives in different nook and cranny of the country. It divulges into details that are hidden and remain secret.

Cannot any one protect and promote true Nepali folk culture? Cannot the position of many Gaines be alleviated in our society? Cannot we hear the pathos and bathos of the poor? Gaines are archives that carry the voice of the marginalized, the poor, the downtrodden, the squatter, and the widow. They play the culture and the practices of different nooks and crannies of the country in the strings of Sarangi. When I am in pain or hear the untimely demise of innocent lives, I muse on the strings of Sarangi. (**Published in *The Himalayan Times* June 30, 2005**)

Tears of Joy

A COUPLE OF DAYS AGO my brother, Cheban, flew to the US for higher studies. I was thrilled because this was the first time that anyone from my family was going abroad for higher studies, that too, by winning a scholarship.

We all became very emotional when the moment of departure arrived. Most of the relatives, friends, and near and dear ones had gathered at the airport. It was indeed a joyous moment. We even took several photographs in order to cherish the moment.

But the most painful experience was when my sister and uncle hugged him tightly and started crying. The occasion became both joyous and painful. I almost froze and could not utter a word. My emotions remained bottled up within me. There was nothing that I could do. However, I secretly kept a cassette in my brother's bag. The cassette contained a few outpourings which I had dubbed a day before. It had a few words of encouragement and inspiration which would come in handy in trying times. I had particularly urged him not to forget his motherland and the Nepali people.

It was he with whom I had passed many wonderful days, months, and years. He is now far away though geographically only. He has crossed many seas and oceans. In fact, he is in an alien world. But the emotional bond between me and my brother is eternal. In his presence, I had never discussed those special ties. But my mind was now flooded with childhood memories. How we used to play "Chor and police" and had our lunch from the same plate. We used to visit most of the places together. I distinctly remember how my brother used to steal sweets from my pocket. Those were the days!

I could not control my tears anymore. I felt as if something had gone missing from my life. But I soon realized that my brother had gone nowhere; rather, he would return after a certain period of time. It was not a painful departure but an initiation into a progressive life. I'm waiting for the moment when I will be reunited with my brother, who will return to his motherland equipped with all the expertise. This is because I had seen tears in the eyes of those who had come to say goodbye. After all, those tears were of joy and not of sorrow. (**Published in** *The Himalayan Times* **August 31, 2005**)

Books by Tulasi Acharya:

MOCHAN: An action-packed Nepali novel on the duality of love, life, and relationship between two continents, leading to meditation and resolution.

Sex, Gender and Disability in Nepal: This book explores the sex lives of women with disabilities in Nepal, showing that many women suffer more than men despite prevailing disability policies that emphasize nondiscrimination against people with disabilities. It also argues that far from general perceptions of women as asexual, women with disabilities are capable of leading highly creative and fulfilling sexual lives.

Running from the Dreamland: "This novel sees America through the eyes of a visiting student from Kathmandu as he struggles to make a life in his new land...Importantly, this story gives us insight into the immigrant experience and the difficulties..."

A Collection of Shakespeare's Stories: The book is a translated-into-Nepali-collection of Shakespeare's stories, originally in English edited by Charles Lamb and Mary Lamb. Translated stories are: The Tempest, A Midsummer Night's dream, The Winter's Tale, Much Ado About Nothing, As You Like It, The Merchant of Venice, Macbeth...

I Won't Marry: These are the poems oozed out of the poet's experience and perception looking at people and the world around him.

Handbook of Professional Writing: This book is divided into two parts. Part one deals with technical topics in writing, such as business writing, proposal writing, writing for research, digital writing and other technical topics in writing, including even technical topics in literature. Part two is entirely on the topic of mass communication and journalism. The second part covers at length the issues and matters relating to mass communication and journalism, theories, and some technical aspect of editing, proofreading, photo editing, reporting, lay-out, broadcasting media, and so on.

Living by Memories

Don't miss out!

Visit the website below and you can sign up to receive emails whenever TULASI ACHARYA publishes a new book. There's no charge and no obligation.

https://books2read.com/r/B-A-RGZU-BTTBC

BOOKS2READ

Connecting independent readers to independent writers.

Also by TULASI ACHARYA

Mochan
Running from the Dreamland
Katai Bomb, Katai Bamjan (??? ??, ??? ?????)
Living by Memories

Watch for more at www.tulasiacharya.com.

About the Author

Tulasi Acharya was born in the South Asian country of Nepal. He completed his Master's degree in English in Tribhuvan University in Kathmandu. He also taught English and Journalism courses at colleges in Nepal, where he authored textbooks on mass communication and journalism. A prolific writer, Acharya published short stories, poems, and articles in Nepali journals, national newspapers and online. He moved to the United States in 2008 to pursue a Master's degree in creative writing. He holds a Ph.D. in Public Administration from Florida Atlantic University, USA. Originally from Nepal, Acharya has a Master's degree in Women's Studies and a degree in Professional Writing. His research interests are disability, policy, gender and sexuality, marginalized narratives, critical theory, and post colonialism, including creative writing and translation.

Read more at www.tulasiacharya.com.